PATERSON & PASSAIC COUNTY

Picture Research by Bromley C. Palamountain

Partners in Progress by Robert J. Masiello

Produced in Cooperation with
The Greater Paterson Chamber of Commerce

Windsor Publications, Inc.
Northridge, California

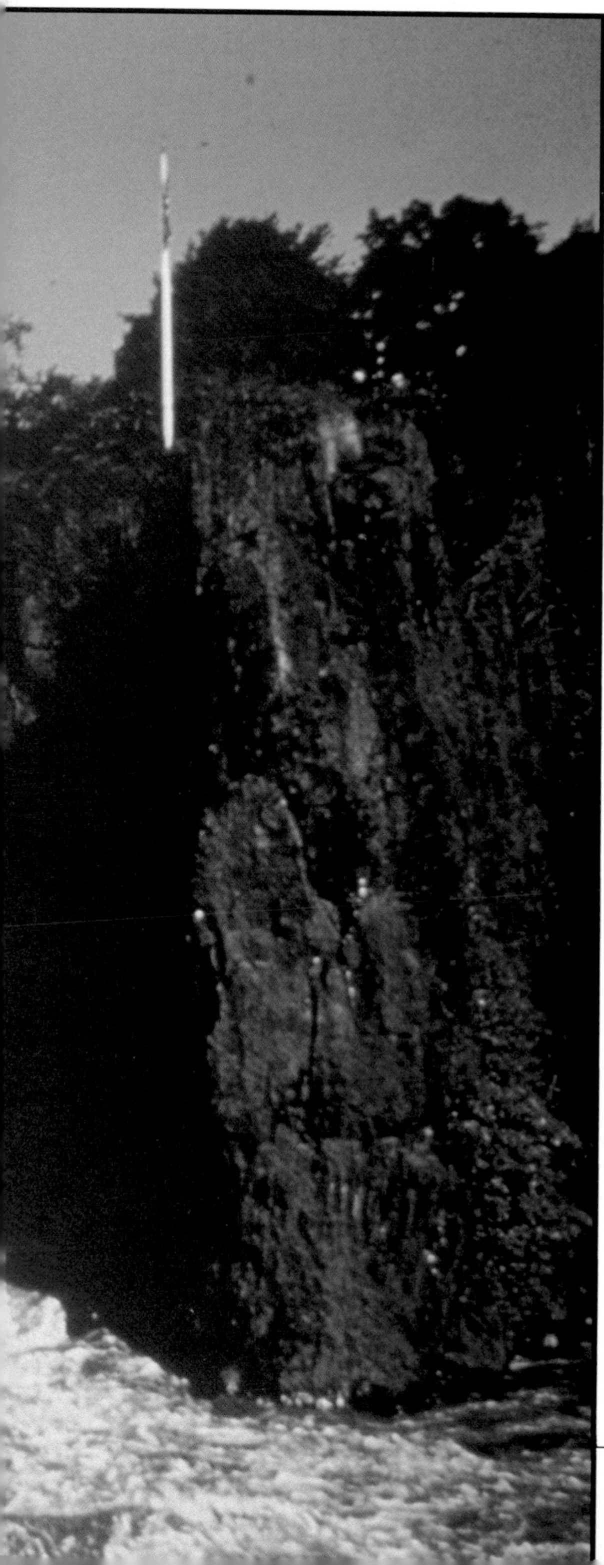

PATERSON & PASSAIC COUNTY

AN ILLUSTRATED HISTORY

By J. Palmer Murphy and Margaret Murphy

Windsor Publications, Inc.—History Book Division

Vice-President of Publishing: Hal Silverman
Editorial Director: Teri Davis Greenberg
Design Director: Alexander E. D'Anca

Staff for *Paterson & Passaic County*

Senior Editor: Susan L. Wells
Director, Corporate Biographies: Karen Story
Assistant Director, Corporate Biographies: Phyllis Gray
Editor, Corporate Biographies: Judith L. Hunter
Production Editor, Corporate Biographies: Una FitzSimons
Layout Artist, Corporate Biographies: Mari Catherine Preimesberger
Sales Representatives, Corporate Biographies: Robert Ottenheimer
Editorial Assistants: Brenda Berryhill, Kathy M. Brown, Laura Cordova, Nina Kanga, Susan Kanga, Susan J. Muhler, Pat Pittman

Designer: Thomas Prager
Layout Artist: Christina McKibbin

Library of Congress Cataloging-in-Publication Data
Murphy, Palmer J., 1915-1986 Paterson & Passaic County. Bibliography: p. Includes index. 1. Paterson (N.J.)—History. 2. Paterson (N.J.)—Description. 3. Paterson (N.J.)—Industries.
4. Passaic County (N.J.)—History. 5. Passaic County (N.J.)—Description and travel. 6. Passaic County (N.J.)—Industries. I. Murphy, Margaret, 1956- .
II. Title. III. Title: Paterson and Passaic County.
F144.P4M86 1987 974.9'23 87-13262
ISBN 0-89781-203-Y

Published 1987
Printed in the United States of America
First Edition

Previous page: Sunlight streaming through the spray of the Great Falls of the Passaic River creates a rainbow effect. Courtesy, New Jersey Department of Travel and Tourism

Facing page: This horsedrawn streetcar was photographed in the 1880s on Broadway at West and Main streets. Courtesy, The Paterson Museum

Front cover: The whole city of Paterson turned out in force to celebrate the city's centennial in 1892. Taken from Colt and Market streets, this photo features a parade of Union Army veterans. Courtesy, The Paterson Museum

Back cover: William C.A. Frerich's Little Falls on the Passaic River *depicts the powerful beauty of the falls in about 1889. Courtesy, Ringwood Manner State Park, Alice and Hamilton Fish Library*

CONTENTS

INTRODUCTION

Facing page: This is a portrait of three salesmen for Ammon & Person Creamery Butterine. What butterine may have been is a mystery in the 1980s, but it was clearly a profit leader. Courtesy, Passaic County Historical Society

The city of Paterson, New Jersey, was founded nearly 200 years ago by an odd assortment of merchant adventurers, financiers, and politicians. Many saw the potential of the city by the Great Falls of the Passaic River and remained with the Society for Establishing Useful Manufactures' project through its first, although shaky, twenty years. Before the SUM, there was nothing but a place called The Swamp, a huge waterfall, and a handful of Dutch and English settlers.

The two centuries that followed have seen the city reach astonishing peaks and suffer near-crushing declines. Always the resilience of Paterson's entrepreneurs, backed by waves of immigrant labor, have brought the city back from the brink.

Paterson's history is therefore inextricably linked with the fortunes of American growth, but always in more intense doses. National crises were unmitigated disasters for Paterson, while times of prosperity brought outright opulance. Yet, Paterson has retained an identity peculiar to itself. There was no original, central core town and most of the city's original citizens throughout the nineteenth century were not American, and in most cases did not claim English as an original language. Meeting this kind of a challenge has demanded people with creativity, wills of iron, and a predeliction for hard work. These sorts of people have always been Paterson's greatest strength, a kind of renewable resource.

Paterson has now reached another crossroads and is moving forward after a series of lean years. The downtown area is rebuilding with exciting new plans for the future. The physical plant of local industry and commerce is expanding almost daily. In short, the city has found new direction.

With the unified commitment of Patersonians and in partnership with her sister townships in both halves of this "hourglass county," Paterson looks with confidence to its future while it preserves its astonishingly rich past.

William C.A. Frerich's Little Falls on the Passaic River *depicts the powerful beauty of the falls in about 1889. Courtesy, Ringwood Manner State Park, Alice and Hamilton Fish Library*

AMMON & PERSON
BABY BRAND
Creamery Butterine
Always
Fresh from
the Churn

Chapter I

The Influence of the Rivers

The story of Passaic County begins with its rivers, five of which have been influential in its history and still play prominent roles today. These rivers, long important to the Indians, later served as highways for explorers and then settlers, who used these routes to bring in their household goods and families, to import supplies, and conduct trade. The rivers afforded protection for the Continental Army in the Revolutionary War, enclosing an area that became known as the Arsenal of the Revolution. The rivers were a significant factor in the establishment of Paterson as the nation's first industrial city, endowed with abundant water power for manufacturing and later for the generation of electricity. The rivers of Passaic County have been suppliers of potable water for millions of people, places for sports and recreation, and boundaries for counties and municipalities.

Notable "firsts" associated with these rivers include the manufacture of the first Colt revolver, "the gun that won the West," and the construction and testing of the first modern submarine. Passaic County's rivers were a tourist and honeymoon attraction long before Niagara Falls became famous.

The five influential rivers all bear Indian names: Passaic, Pompton, Pequannock, Wanaque, and Ramapo. Some modern spellings of Indian names are attributable to the difficulty the early Dutch and English settlers had in translating and transcribing them into their languages. The early English attempts to use phonetics added to the confusion in legal documents. There have been at least fifteen accepted spellings and possible derivations for the word *Passaic* and seven for *Pequannock*. Scholars have counted no less than eighty-three spellings for Ackquackanonk, one of the earliest settlements in the area. Problems with Indian names still linger. For example, the river, borough, and reservoir named Wanaque are pronounced by inhabitants, neighbors, county officials, and others as *Wana Q*, *Wan-Akey* or *Wynockey*. *Wanakey* seems to be the most common.

Other place names in the area are easier to trace. Some originated with notable persons: as Paterson was named for the governor of New Jersey, William Paterson, and Charlottesburg for the consort of King George III, who lost his American realm partly because of the iron mined and forged in the village named for her. Little Falls and Clifton were named for geological formations, and Wayne for Revolutionary War general Anthony Wayne. Bloomingdale

Facing Page: The Old Nail Factory near the Great Falls was painted by Thomas Whitley. Nails were originally cut by hand, which made them so valuable that they were used as money. The overshot waterwheel shown in this factory increased productivity and lowered the cost of nails. Courtesy, Passaic County Historical Society

The Pequannock River near Mountain View was photographed in about 1900. Courtesy, Passaic County Historical Society

was the inspiration of a promoter who thought the name's pleasant connotation would attract tourists and residents. Several places were named for areas in Europe, reminding settlers of old homelands and a different life. Passaic, Pompton Lakes, and Wanaque were named for their rivers, as was Pequannock in Morris County.

Of all the water courses in the county, the Passaic River is most significant. Into it flow all the others, including the Peckman River, which now is little more than a creek flowing through Little Falls. Long ago it provided water power for gristmills and tanneries. Today, it is almost dry in times of drought, yet can become a raging torrent during floods.

Many small tributaries feed the Passaic within the county boundaries, such as the Singac, Molly Ann, Weasel, and Oldham brooks. There is one small stream, now almost obliterated, that for a brief moment had an odd role in Passaic County history. In Notch Brook, at Little Falls in 1857, a Paterson carpenter named Jacob Quackenbush was dredging for freshwater mussels and found one containing a large pink pearl, which, legend says, he sold to Tiffany's in New York for $1,500. The pearl was set in the crown of Empress Eugenie of France. The event created Passaic County's version of a gold rush, as thousands of local residents as well as many from New York flocked to the brook to hunt for pearls. Approximately $15,000 worth of pearls were taken from the brook that year, drastically reducing the mussel population. Few, if any, pearls have been found there in the past 125 years.

The Passaic is also the longest river in the state, measuring ninety miles on a corkscrew course through seven counties before it joins the Hackensack to form Newark Bay and become part of New York Harbor. Despite its meandering, it enters the Atlantic Ocean less than twenty-five miles as the crow flies from its point of origin. The river also takes on water from many other streams and marshes in Somerset, Morris, Essex, and Bergen counties, and enters Passaic County in Wayne Township at Mountain View. There it joins the Pompton River, which has already taken in the waters of the Ramapo, Wanaque, and Pequannock, and becomes a majestic placid stream until it reaches Little Falls.

At Singac, the northernmost village in Little Falls Township, the New York and Greenwood Lake Railroad built a station where many excursionists, weary of the twenty-seven stops on the run from Jersey City to Greenwood Lake, left the train to enjoy swimming, boating, and fishing. This area was also used for location shooting of many famous early movies, such as *The Perils of Pauline* and *The Great Train Robbery*.

The Little Falls, for which the township was named, were never as precipitous a drop as the Great Falls in Paterson but sloped gently in a half-mile roaring cascade that lowered the elevation of the river by fifty-one feet. At one time the river was 300 feet wide and ten feet deep, but that is scarcely true today. One reason was that the cascade ran over valuable brownstone, which was quarried and used in the construction of the famous Trinity Church as well as the characteristic brownstone houses in New York. Also reducing the flow over the Little Falls was a dam, later called Beattie's Dam, first erected at the top of the falls more than two centuries ago for iron, grist, and sawmills. The dam was later used to provide water for Paterson, Passaic, and Clifton, since the river at Little Falls has never been as polluted as it became below the Great Falls at Paterson. Today the Passaic Valley Water Commission operates a large filtration plant at Little Falls.

Many people mistake the site of Beattie's Dam for the Little Falls because the dam is built around a natural rock ledge in the river creating a spectacular cascade in flood times. However, the true falls were below the present dam.

After its descent at Little Falls, the river winds placidly to West Paterson and into Paterson, where it reaches its most famous form as the Great Falls of the Passaic. With a perpendicular drop of seventy-seven feet, it is by most measurements second only to the falls at Niagara as the largest waterfall east of the Mississippi River.

Perhaps the most momentous day in the history of the Great Falls was July 10, 1778. On that date General George Washington and his aide-de-camp, Colonel Alexander Hamilton, enjoyed a picnic lunch at the base of the falls. The general was already familiar with the area and appreciated it from a military point of view, but Hamilton was viewing the falls for the first time and was greatly impressed by them as a source of water power. About a dozen years later, as Washington's secretary of the treasury, Hamilton remembered the locale as he laid plans to create the Society for Useful Manufactures (SUM) and the beginnings of an industrial economy in the United States.

Legend holds that Washington, Hamilton, and other staff officers, while having lunch at the falls that day, "drank Madiera wine and gamboled with the local maidens." Lawrence A. Trumbull, in his 1882 *History of Industrial Paterson,* asserts that Washington's and Hamilton's initials were carved in the rock and still visible in that year.

There have been other momentous days around the falls occasioned by tightrope walks over the gorge, the launching of the first submarine, the founding of the SUM, the dedication of the falls as a national monument by President Gerald Ford, and many other festivities.

In Indian and colonial days the Passaic River was one of the finest fisheries in the Northeast. From Newark to Passaic it was noted for great numbers of shad. Sturgeon ran as heavy as 130 pounds. Bass, pickerel, perch, and trout were caught in abundance prior to the Civil War.

Unfortunately, by the late nineteenth century, the river had become polluted. Its waters were unfit for fish. Downriver from the Great Falls, the Passaic had become a veritable open sewer. Into it poured the waste from industrial facilities, in addition to sewage from the many municipalities with their growing populations. During the drought of 1894, the acidic fumes from the lower Passaic caused the paint on houses

Right: William Paterson was governor of New Jersey after the American Revolution. The new city was named after him in recognition of his service. Courtesy, Mid-Lantic Bank/North

Below: The two falls systems on the Passaic River were made-to-order for landscape painters. In this oil painting of the Great Falls, done in about 1830, the artist painted out the nearby factories and mills. Courtesy, Passaic County Historical Society

Colored lithographs of the Great Falls were popular in Europe, as this 1840s French print suggests. Courtesy, Passaic County Historical Society

along the river to peel and blister.

At the turn of the century, efforts to clean up the river got off to a fitful start. The Passaic Valley Trunk Sewer Commission, established by law in 1902, was for many years unable to undertake this task, owing to litigation brought by New York State and the City of Paterson. By 1924, the trunk sewer was completed, running along the west side of the Passaic River from the Great Falls to a pumping station in Newark Bay and then to an outflow in New York Harbor at Robbins Reef. Presently operated by the Passaic Valley Sewerage Commission, and assisted by the Army Corps of Engineers, which deepened the river channel, it has gone far in reducing the pollution of the stream. In the last decade communities along the lower river have taken vigorous steps to clean up the banks and river. At present it is once again a recreational resource, with boat clubs reactivated and new parks created. Crews now skull on the river, and while the fish have not returned in large numbers, it is now a much more attractive stream than it was twenty years ago.

Shipping has declined in importance during the same twenty years but remains a significant part of the history of the Passaic River, which is tidal and navigable, having a dredged channel, from Newark Bay

These workmen were photographed building the windface of the Clinton Reservoir dam in the 1890s. All the materials came from nearby quarries. Courtesy, Passaic County Historical Society

Building the windface of Macopin Dam in upper Passaic County in the 1800s utilized steam shovels, the most advanced technological tools available to the builders. This etching originally appeared in Harper's Weekly. *Courtesy, Vincent Marchese*

to the City of Passaic.

The first steamboat operated in the western hemisphere was the *Polacca,* built and launched on the Passaic River in what is now Belleville, Essex County, on October 21, 1798. Sixty feet long, the *Polacca* was constructed at the foundry of Nicholas J. Roosevelt. It was the brainchild of John Stevens of Hoboken, who also pioneered bringing railroads and improved highways to the nation. To prove the power of steam he ran the first steam locomotive on a circular track on the lawn of his estate in Hoboken. Stevens Institute of Technology, whose campus encompasses his former estate, is named in memory of his family.

From his writings it is clear that Stevens had a hatred of the uncomfortable travel by stagecoach from Jersey City to Philadelphia, a two-day trip he often made on business. After having been bounced unbearably through the marshes around the Hackensack River, he built a plank road to smooth that part of the trip. Then, crossing the Hackensack, Passaic, and Raritan rivers, he concluded that if ships did not have to depend on a following wind and an ebb tide to reach their destinations downriver, the trip would be considerably smoother. So he turned to steamboats. The *Polacca* was his first effort, and it proved to be a modified success. On her trial run, the *Polacca* traveled at three-and-one-half miles per hour on the Passaic and steamed on to New York, according to Harry Emerson Wildes in *Twin Rivers: The Raritan and the Passaic.*

Passaic County's water resources have been developed to provide power for factories, recreation, and water supplies for the Newark metropolitan area. Pictured here in the 1880s is the building of the dam at the Oakwood Reservoir. Courtesy, Vincent Marchese

Unfortunately, the *Polacca* proved unseaworthy.

Stevens built bigger and better boats for commercial service, thus creating a legal confrontation that eventually had to be decided by the United States Supreme Court. New York State had granted a monopoly for operation of steamboats in New York waters to Robert Fulton. New Jersey granted a similar monopoly to Stevens and his associates, including New Jersey Governor Aaron Odgen, Thomas Gibbons, and "Commodore" Cornelius Vanderbilt, subsequently the guiding light of the New York Central Railroad. Under the monopolies, New Jersey ferryboats could not dock in New York, nor could New York boats dock in New Jersey. Thus began what many historians call "The Ferryboat War," a court battle that became more and more complicated as various parties to the action changed sides frequently. Stevens was no longer actively involved when the final solution was reached in Chief Justice John Marshall's landmark decision *Gibbons* v. *Ogden*, which determined that the United States Constitution permitted free use of interstate waters for commerce. This opening of the waterways brought on a cutthroat price war: Vanderbilt offered passage from New Brunswick to New York, including a sumptuous dinner, for six cents. The Stevens family soon bought out Vanderbilt, who used the proceeds to get into the railroad business.

Robert Fulton, with his 1807 launch of the *Clermont* is credited in many history books as the first to bring steam navigation to this hemisphere and as the Father of the Steamboat, even though Stevens launched the *Polacca* in 1798, when Fulton was still in Europe.

Toward the end of the century the Passaic River was the scene of another maritime first—the launch of the prototype modern submarine, powered by an internal-combustion engine rather than by the crew. John P. Holland, a mathematics teacher in a Paterson high school, tested his submersible boat in the river just above the Great Falls in June 1887. Holland took the two-ton craft twelve feet below the surface and remained down for more than sixty minutes, cruising at up to four miles per hour. That submarine is now on view at The Paterson Museum, which also houses many of Holland's papers. The U.S. Navy's first submarine—commissioned in 1900 as the USS *Holland*—was named for the Passaic County inventor and was a direct descendant of the submersible first demonstrated in the Passaic River.

The Wanaque is the smallest river in the country and the only one that runs its entire course within Passaic County. Although small, it provides the area's greatest impoundment of water in the Wanaque Reservoir, which has a capacity of thirty billion gallons. With additional water pumped to it via pipelines from the Ramapo River at Pompton Lakes, the reservoir has a system of eight dams, the largest being the Raymond Dam, which is 1,500 feet long.

The Pequannock River originates in Sussex County and flows into the Pompton at Pompton Lakes, serving for a long portion of its route as the boundary between Morris and Passaic counties. In 1892 the river became the source of potable water for the City of Newark and its customer municipalities. Prior to 1892 Newark drew water from the Passaic River as it passed the Newark city limits, where pollution and annual epidemics of typhoid fever caused Newark to seek an alternate source. Pequannock River water flowed through the taps of Newark residents for the first time on January 12, 1892, and by a court decision in 1900 the entire Pequannock Watershed, with a capacity of eleven billion gallons, was turned over to the Newark Watershed. In Passaic County the Pequannock has been dammed for four Newark reservoirs: Oak Ridge, Clinton, Charlottesburg, and Macopin, all in the northern part of the county. When the Morris Canal was in operation, the Pequannock and the Pompton rivers were feeders maintaining the water level in the canal.

The Ramapo River runs for only a short distance in Passaic County, most of its course being in neighboring Bergen County and in New York State. It joins the Wanaque to form the Pompton at Pompton Lakes borough, where a high dam forms Pompton Lake. The dam was used at one time to furnish water for iron-smelting furnaces and subsequently to generate electricity. Today the chief activity is recreation—swimming, boating, fishing, and ice skating.

Another major recreational area, and Passaic County's largest body of water other than reservoirs, is Greenwood Lake, near the New York State border. In colonial days this was iron country, dotted with mines, forges, and furnaces. In 1768 Baron Hasenclever, the ironmaster of the Ringwood area, built a dam five feet high and 200 feet long to create what he called Long Pond, enabling him to store water from rainy seasons for use in his ironworks in the dry seasons. It became Greenwood Lake after 1834 when Morris Canal interests, seeking to ensure a supply of water for the canal, raised the dam to twelve feet, doubling the size of the lake and backing the waters up six miles into New York State. Although it was never used as a major water supply for the canal, Greenwood Lake became so popular as a resort that the New

This peaceful scene was carefully posed and shot somewhere in upper Passaic County between 1880 and 1890. Courtesy, Passaic County Historical Society

New Jersey has more covered bridges than any other state. They protected travelers, prevented the spooking of cattle and horses, and shed the heavy winter snows that might otherwise cause a collapse. The bridge shown here was once upstream from Little Falls. Courtesy, Vincent Marchese

York and Greenwood Lake Railroad was charted to run through Essex, Morris, and Passaic counties, bringing swarms of "day trippers" for an outing in the country. It is still a summer resort for many, although more have been building year-round homes there. The lake covers 1,920 acres and drains into the Wanaque River.

Despite their benefits to the region, the rivers are all given to major flooding, as are their tributaries. The greatest flood in the Passaic Basin occurred in October 1903. The Army Corps of Engineers described it as a "once in a century flood" caused by rainfall. The summer of 1903 had been a wet one, with rainfall six inches above normal. Reservoirs were full and rivers high. Between October 8 and 11, 1903, the basin was deluged with 11.74 inches of rain; the measurement in Paterson between October 7 and 9 was 15.04 inches. Every river ran high over its banks. The Passaic crested fifteen feet above flood stage in Paterson. The southern portion of Passaic County was devastated, as were large portions of Bergen and Essex counties.

There had long been talk of flood control projects for the basin, especially in years following a severe flood, as in December 1878 and February 1902. State action in creating the North Jersey Flood Commission, the Passaic River Flood District Commission, and the State Water Supply Commission failed to remedy the flood problems. After a flood in 1936, Congress authorized the Army Corps of Engineers to make a preliminary survey, but there was little progress toward the goal of a flood control project until floods again occurred in the late 1940s and the 1950s. Finally the Corps of Engineers drew up several plans, but none could be found that satisfied everyone, as the various counties, localities, and interests battled each other. Meanwhile, the flooding continues. The most recent severe floods, in April 1984, left hundreds homeless and caused damage estimated in the millions.

The Army Corps of Engineers' current plan calls for a huge tunnel, acting as an underground bypass, to be built from the Passaic River at the Little Falls-Wayne area to a downstream site in Essex County, below the Second River. Although some objections have been raised by residents in Essx County, the proposal is moving toward implementation as the need for flood control becomes ever more acute. Today a flood smaller than that of 1903 causes more damage than that big one, beause since that time homes and shops have been built in the floodplain, and much of the swampland, which absorbed some of the water, has been paved over. Today, areas such as major highways bordering the river, previously unaffected, are becoming subject to flooding and making flood conrol a critical priority for the future of the basin.

For good and for ill, the rivers have had their influence on the development of Passaic County. For many centuries they have wound their way to the sea, bearing witness for only the past few hundred years to the human history of Passaic County.

Chapter II

The Original People

It is a common misconception that North America was teeming with Indians before the arrival of the first explorers. This idea was nurtured by early artists who depicted Columbus, Hudson, and even the Pilgrims, being greeted by large bands of "savages" upon their arrival in the new land.

There were probably only 10,000 Indians living within New Jersey's present boundaries when Henry Hudson and his crew were met by a group of tribesmen in Sandy Hook Bay. By 1700 this number had dwindled to 500.

The Indians who lived in the area that would become New Jersey were Leni-Lenape or "original people," a branch of the Algonquin tribe. They were later called the Delawares, after the river along which many of them lived. There were three major divisions of the Leni-Lenape: the Unalachtigo, located in the southern part of the state; the Unami, in the central section; and the Minsi, in the north. Each had its own totem (turkey for the Unalachtigo, turtle for the Unami, and wolf for the Minsi) and spoke its own dialect.

The Minsi were the most militant, while the Leni-Lenape were a peaceful and stable people. As they demonstrated to the European settlers, they would fight in retaliation but generally did not attack unless provoked. Moreover, their traditions dictated hospitality toward stangers. In his *Account of the Leni-Lenape or Delaware Indians* (1683), William Penn described their courtesy: "If an European comes to see them, or calls for lodging at their house or wigwam, they give him the best place and first cut." Among the Leni-Lenape, Penn said, "nothing is too good for their friend."

Other tribes called them "Old Women" because of their lack of belligerence. This may have been a compliment, as older women sometimes played a key role in inter-tribal negotiations, and the Leni-Lenape were arbitrators in Indian disputes. In any case, they were known as peacemakers rather than warriors.

Many of the earliest passages through the county and state were rivers and streams. The Leni-Lenape used these waterways for travel as well as for fishing. Both water and land trails were used not only by Indians living within the state, but by tribes in New York and Pennsylvania who made annual excursions to the coast for what may have been the first "clambakes." While plenty of freshwater fish was available, seafood, especially clams and oysters, was a delicacy. Another benefit was collecting shells to be

Facing page: Leni-Lenape Indians used spears to hunt game for food. This John T. Kraft drawing shows an atlatl, *a spear-thrower that was used to increase the accuracy and force of the weapon. Courtesy, Herbert C. Kraft*

carried back and made into wampum. Some Leni-Lenape charged a fee for passage to the shore and for the fishing, thus becoming New Jersey's first practitioners of tourism.

Some of the Leni-Lenape were nomadic, cultivating a crop and then moving on according to a pattern of growing and hunting seasons. Others lived in more permanent settlements, one of the largest of which was located on land that is now part of Passaic. This Passaic group may have been less nomadic than others because of the abundant food supply. Shad and eel were plentiful, and the area below the Great Falls was particularly good for fishing. Remains of the stone dams used to catch fish could be seen along the Passaic River as late as 1920. A variety of game was available in the woods nearby. The Leni-Lenape also gathered fruits and nuts for food as well as plants and herbs for medicinal purposes. In addition to hunting and fishing, the Leni-Lenape grew a variety of crops, including squash, pumpkin, beans, and maize. A mainstay of the diet, maize was roasted, boiled, or made into cakes.

The Passaic village, inhabited by approximately 500 Leni-Lenape, was typical in its layout of family homes around a ceremonial center. In the vicinity of present-day Garfield was a larger gathering place used by the Passaic villagers and other Leni-Lenape groups for ceremonial dances and sporting events. Horse and boat races were held there. This was also a place for religious ceremony. The Leni-Lenape religion centered around worship of a supreme being, Manitou, with other spirits acting as guardian angels for individual Leni-Lenape. They believed that after death the spirit would go on to a utopian afterlife. Part of their worship involved a ceremony William Penn described as the *cantico,* performed with singing and dancing and sacrifice of crops and game. The local place-name *Yanticaw* is thought to be a corruption of the Leni-Lenape word *canticaw,* or place for dancing.

In the social organization of the Leni-Lenape, both men and women worked in some way to support the family. Hunting was strictly an activity for males. Women were sometimes allowed to participate in fishing expeditions, but generally their role was to grow crops and gather other food.

Leni-Lenape usually married at a young age. The men were seventeen or eighteen years old when they married, and the women were three to four years younger. The woman was the initiator in seeking a spouse. When she was ready to marry, she would create a headpiece, sometimes made from feathers. Parents arranged marriages with tacit consent of their children. According to Penn, once a couple married, the husband was in charge and the wife assumed the role of servant to him, although "the men are very affectionate." If either spouse became displeased with the other, departure constituted divorce. The woman automatically had custody of the children if this happened, as raising them was seen as being a woman's province.

"Industry" in the area later to become Passaic County began with the Leni-Lenape, who ran a wampum "factory" in Passaic. White Wampum was made from the whorls of conch shells. White beads were worth about half as much as the black ones, which were made from clam shells. The shells had to be ground, polished, and drilled so that they could be strung and carried as money or worn as decoration. There was close proximity to a plentiful supply of the shells and a sufficient number of people to perform the labor. Settlers from Europe later set up their own wampum operations, notably a Dutch family named Stolts that made wampum at Goffle Hill (Hawthorne) between 1700 and 1770.

When the first Europeans arrived, the Leni-Lenape were a small but flourishing tribe with established villages, social customs, religion, and a variety of communal and economic traditions that brought in

The Leni-Lenape Indians were New Jersey's first fishermen. This fishing party is depicted hauling in the day's catch, while previous catches are being prepared by smoking, cooking, and drying. Drawing by John T. Kraft, courtesy, Herbert C. Kraft

both food and furs for trade. Perhaps the earliest account of them comes from Giovanni de Varrazano, who in 1524 encountered Indians who are believed to have been Leni-Lenape because of their peacefulness and welcoming attitude. John T. Cunningham, in *New Jersey, America's Main Road*, quotes Verrazano's description:

They came without fear aboard our ship. This is the goodliest people and of the fairest conditions that we have found in this our voyage. They exceed us in bigness, they are the colour of brass, some of them inclined more to whiteness, others are of yellow colour, of comely visage with long and black hair, which they are very careful to trim and deck up. They are black and quick eyed, and of sweet and pleasant countenance, imitating much the old fashion . . . The women are of like conformity and beauty, very handsome and well favored, of pleasant countenance, and comely to behold; they are as well mannered and continent as any women, and of good education; they are all naked save a cover of deer skin.

In 1609, Henry Hudson's expedition aboard the *Half Moon* was recorded in the journal of Robert Juet, who described the initial meeting with the Indians: "This day the people of the country came aboard of us, seeming very glad of our coming, and brought green tobacco, and gave us of it for knives and beads. They go in deer skins loose, well dressed. They have yellow copper. They desire clothes and are very civil."

A few days later a crew member venturing out in a small boat was killed by local Indians. Juet relates that while the Indians continued coming aboard the *Half Moon*, seeming friendly and interested in trade, the sailors never trusted them again. Relations with natives on both sides of the river deteriorated, and before sailing off the *Half Moon* fired on and killed several Indians.

Generally, the members of the early expeditions made an effort to establish and maintain good relations with the natives. The goal of the Dutch West India Company was to profit through trade, and trade was not fostered by fighting. Moreover, the Dutch West India Company made no attempt to convert the Indians, as their interest was purely economic.

The Indians proved valuable to the Europeans in new ways with the arrival of the first settlers in the early seventeenth century. The Dutch and English who came to the New World to live were unfamiliar not only with the geography but also with crops that could be grown successfully in this area and with the herbs that could be used medicinally. The Europeans retained their practice of hunting with guns but did adopt Leni-Lenape fishing methods. Since the early settlers lived in small vulnerable groups, it was to their advantage to cultivate the good will of the Indians.

Unfortunately, as the settlers became acclimated and grew in numbers, disputes began to arise. Their dependence on Indian knowledge lessened, and their increasing needs for land and resources came into conflict with the Leni-Lenape's needs. The places on which the Indians had chosen to settle were attractive to the Europeans for the same basic reasons—proximity to waterways for travel and fishing, and richness of soil for agriculture. Conflicts arose over cultural and religious differences, and some were worsened by the Indians' inexperience with alcohol. The trading of rum for furs often led to quarrels and sometimes to violence. Racial prejudice on the part of the Europeans also worsened the problems. The most frequent misunderstandings, though, concerned property transactions.

The concept of land ownership was unknown among the Leni-Lenape. A tribe did not own land but rather held rights to hunt or fish on a certain piece of land. If necessary, the rights could be purchased from another tribe for a designated period of time. The Indians apparently believed that they were selling only these rights to the Europeans, who thought they were purchasing land in a typical European sense. This difference led to serious problems, as the Indians strongly resented not being able to return later and use the land. After some time, as communication between the Europeans and Indians became easier, the Leni-Lenape came to understand what the Europeans meant in a land purchase. In 1832, a Princeton-educated Indian, Bartolomew S. Calvin, whose Leni-Lenape name meant Wilted Grass, lobbied the state legislature to pay for lands the Leni-Lenape had given up for trinkets. The legislature paid the full amount requested—$2,000—to Wilted Grass.

The grievances between Indians and Europeans sometimes escalated to warfare. One of the worst attacks was made by the Dutch on an Indian settlement at Communipaw, near the site of present-day Jersey City. Governor Willem Kieft, determined to respond to scattered raids by the Indians, ordered the surprise attack on Communipaw, which turned into a massacre as eighty Indians were killed. The Indians retaliated, and thus the Indian War of 1643 began. Much of the fighting took place near Passaic County.

The situation between the Indians and the settlers improved somewhat when the British took over. Their official policy toward the Leni-Lenape, summed up in the colonial proprietors' instructions to Governor Philip Carteret in 1664, was to "treat them with all humanity and kindness and not in any wise grieve or oppress them; but endeavoring, by Christian Carriage, to manifest Piety, Justice and Charity in your conversation with them." The motivation here was not entirely altruistic, since this course of action would "prove beneficial to the Planters, and likewise Advantageous to the Propagation of the Gospel." As did the Dutch when they first settled, the British wanted to avoid provoking the Indians to attack. In subsequent years British behavior toward the Leni-Lenape was governed by the general principle of benefit to the British. Depending on the needs of the moment, treatment of the Indians ranged from recognizing Leni-Lenape tribal custom as law to holding Leni-Lenape as slaves.

In this John T. Kraft sketch, Leni-Lenape Indians are shown in a burial scene, preparing to wrap the deceased in tree bark. Courtesy, Herbert C. Kraft

Ultimately, the Leni-Lenape were eliminated from Passaic County, and all of the state. War was responsible for some of their decline, and lack of resistance to European diseases such as smallpox led to epidemics that ravaged the population. The remaining Indians were forced out by the continued influx of European population and the introduction of grazing animals, which required more and more land. By the beginning of the eighteenth century, there were probably no more than 500 Leni-Lenape in the state, most of whom moved on to the first U.S. Indian reservation located at Brotherton.

The legacy of the Indians is plainly seen in many place names, such as Passaic, Totowa, Pompton, and Hackensack. The Leni-Lenape influenced the location of European settlements, either by the success of their own settlements or by their work as guides for the newcomers. The Leni-Lenape, having established a system of trails along the easiest routes, allowing for the minimum of hill climbing and stream crossing, must be credited as the early planners of many later roads, including the Hamburg Turnpike. These remnants of their heritage serve as regular reminders of the county's first dwellers.

Chapter III

The Colonists

Facing page: This early Dutch farmhouse was built in 1786 by Uriah Van Riper in Wayne. Courtesy, Passaic County Historical Society

Through the mid-seventeenth century, New Jersey and New York made up a Dutch colony called New Netherland. While the Dutch were very active trading and settling in New York, the number of Europeans living in New Jersey was probably no more than 200, and only two settlements large enough to be called villages were established. Not until the 1670s would anyone other than the Leni-Lenape settle near the Great Falls.

Events were taking place in England, though, that would affect New Jersey's future. In 1660 Charles II, on regaining the British throne, granted to his brother James, Duke of York, all of the land between the Delaware and Connecticut rivers. This area contained most of colonized North America, including the Dutch-held New Netherland. (The English claim to North America was based on the voyage of John Cabot in 1497.) James in turn gave the area between the Hudson and Delaware rivers to two friends—John, Lord Berkeley, and Sir George Carteret—for the token rent of "one pepper corne," to be paid annually. James made this grant out of gratitude for their loyalty during the Civil War, but he also benefited by having someone else develop the area into income-producing property. The name Nova Cesarea was chosen in honor of Carteret's homeland, the Isle of Jersey. Nova Cesarea translates as New Jersey.

In 1664 Britain sent ships and a governor, Richard Nicolls, to enforce its claim to the territory held by the Dutch. Peter Stuyvesant, the governor of New Netherland, wanted to fight but found himself alone in this desire, as most of the Dutch colonists were dissatisfied with the way the Dutch West India Company was handling the settlements. The Dutch West India Company had been established to trade with the Indians, not to develop the area, and so had never shown much concern about the settlers' problems. Since they were outnumbered and outgunned, Dutch residents concluded that fighting was a poor risk when their situation might even be improved by a British takeover.

In some ways British government was beneficial for the Dutch settlers, as it encouraged immigration and development. Berkeley and Carteret, as proprietors of the colony, wished to make New Jersey as attractive as possible, drawing people who would become residents and pay quitrents.

With this in mind, Berkeley and Carteret issued their Concessions and Agreements in 1665. This document ensured freedom of religion, offered land to substantial settlers

Peter Stuyvesant was the first governor of New Netherland, of which Passaic County was once a part. From Ouerta, Long Island Story, 1929

who brought provisions and slaves to the territory, and set up a governmental system that gave each town the right to elect representatives to the assembly. In return for these benefits, the Concessions and Agreements exacted two requirements: a pledge of faithfulness to the king and proprietors and payment of quitrents. Some non-English settlers objected to the pledge of faithfulness. The quitrent system also caused friction.

The two proprietors appointed Philip Carteret, a cousin of Sir George, to be their governor, not knowing that Richard Nicolls had been acting as governor over all of the former New Netherland territory, including New Jersey, and had been granting land patents. On his side, Nicolls did not know about the proprietorship of Berkeley and Carteret. When the proprietors insisted that settlers obtain patents from them and pay quitrents, many refused, saying they had purchased their land from the Indians and received grants from Nicolls.

Trouble began when the first quitrent payment became due in 1670. The Dutch settlers, particularly in the larger towns, rebelled against payment until 1672, when Holland and England officially went to war. Through a surprise appearance of the Dutch fleet in New York harbor in 1673, the Dutch regained control of the colony for a year, returning it to England in 1674 as part of the Treaty of Westminster.

Dutch settlers who agreed to the terms of the Concessions and Agreements were not adversely affected by the return to British rule. They retained their property and experienced the benefits of growth and development if they paid the designated quitrent.

The territory was split into East and West Jersey in 1674-1676, when Berkeley sold his interest to John Fenwick. Carteret retained ownership of East Jersey, which he held until his death in 1681, when East Jersey was then sold to a group of twelve Quakers, one of whom was William Penn. This group appointed Robert Barclay, a Scottish Quaker, as governor. Barclay encouraged hundreds of people, many of them Scots, to emigrate to Jersey. He was not one of them, though; instead Thomas Rudyard acted as an on-site deputy governor.

The government continued to be one of compromise between self-rule by the settlers and control by the proprietors. The twelve proprietors who purchased East Jersey from the Carteret family each took a partner so that the number of proprietors grew to twenty-four. These proprietors soon began to sell portions of their land to others so that by 1688 there were at least seventy-five proprietors.

As provided in the Concessions and Agreements, annual elections were held so that each town was represented at the general assembly. This assembly was also attended by the governor and his council. The proprietors maintained their control by reserving the right of approval over all laws the assembly formed. Any laws this assembly enacted also had to be consistent with English law.

Many settlers from other parts of the

New World were attracted to the area, some with the hope of improving their standard of living, and some looking for religious freedom. Real estate trading was active during the proprietary period, and a large number of patents were granted.

One of the many people interested in available land was Hartmann Michielson, who, like the majority of early settlers in the area, did not arrive directly from Europe but came from another part of the colonies, in his case from the New Jersey town of Bergen. He most probably traveled by the easiest method of transportation available, sailing up the Passaic River. His goal was to establish a post for trading with the Leni-Lenape for furs. Toward this goal, Michielson purchased Dundee (or Menehenicke) Island in the Passaic River from the Leni-Lenape chief Captahen Peeters in 1678. (In the late 1800s dumping into the Passaic River near the island created an artificial extension which joined the island to the mainland.)

Michielson's post, more convenient to the Leni-Lenape than was distant Manhattan, became a success. Apparently convinced of the value of the area, in 1679 Michielson bought 278 acres, the Point Patent land, from Christopher Hoagland, who had purchased it from the Indians.

Hartmann Michielson had been shown the area by Jacques Cortelyou of Manhattan, the first white explorer to see the land. The first recorded description of the Great Falls was written by Jasper Dankers and Peter Sluyter, members of a small mystical sect called the Labadists who wished to leave Europe due to persecution. They described the falls and surrounding area in glowing terms, but eventually the sect settled in New York.

Not long after his Point Patent purchase, Michielson was instrumental in putting together a much larger land deal. He led a group of fourteen in buying approximately 10,000 acres covering land where parts of Clifton, Passaic, and most of Paterson are now located. Joining Hartmann Michielson in this purchase were Hans Diderick, Garrett Garettson, Walling Jacobs, Elias Machielson, Johannes Machielson, Cornelius Machielson, Adrian Post, Urian Tomasen, Cornelius Rowlofson, Symon Jacobs, John Hendrick Speare, Cornelius Lubber, and Abraham Bookey. As the fourteen had made the initial purchase from the Indians and agreed to pay fourteen pounds sterling annually in quitrent, the proprietors granted them a patent in 1684. This piece of land was known as the Ackquackanonk Patent.

In 1683, surrounded by discontent and rebellion in nearby areas, the Ackquackanonk purchasers moved onto their land. Each settler or family was given a lot selected by random drawing. These 100-acre lots were laid out as rectangles along the Passaic so as to allow a maximum number river footage. Some of the borders along these tracts became roads that still exist today. One example, cited by William Nelson, is Willis Street in Paterson. Some of the Ackquackanonk Patentees later bought adjoining land and used this same method, common among the Dutch, of laying out rectangular lots to be randomly selected.

After the original lots were divided among the buyers, some land was set aside for a church and a cemetery. The remainder was split up in subsequent subdivisions as more settlers joined the original families.

Rebellions by the inhabitants of New Jersey eventually became unmanageable for the proprietors. In 1702 they returned the authority to govern the colony to the British Crown. East and West Jersey were united and joined with New York under a royal governor, Lord Cornbury, appointed by Queen Anne. From 1702 until the time of the Revolution, there was a struggle in New Jersey to combine the self-government that the towns had become used to with the royal colonial administration, which was more interested and responsive than the

The mill pond at Ringwood Manor State Park was the scene of much iron ore mining activity in the nineteenth century. It is now popular with tourists, historians, and nature lovers. Courtesy, Vincent Marchese

Cornelius Vreeland established the Notch Inn in this stone house in about 1793 to attract the trade of teamsters hauling pig iron from northern New Jersey mines to Ackquackanonk Landing. The house once served as General St. Clair's headquarters during the American Revolution. Courtesy, Herbert A. Fisher Collection, Julius Forstmann Library

proprietors had been but was also more restrictive.

Against this backdrop of government change and growth, the Passaic County area continued to develop. The Ackquackanonk Tract settlement soon took on an important role since it was situated on the spot where the Passaic River became navigable to Manhattan. It maintained this importance until a railroad line, the Erie, was completed in 1836, lessening the need for water transport of people and goods.

The pattern of European settlements followed in the Leni-Lenape's footsteps. Most of the villages were located close to rivers, which the Europeans, like the Leni-Lenape, used as a resource of water, fish, and transportation. Much of the best land for farming was located on the riverbanks. Well into the eighteenth century, the rivers continued to be the preferred method of travel, because roads were few and difficult to keep in good repair. By the time of the Revolution, still only one stage route served the area. Once a week it ran from Godwin's Tavern in present-day Paterson, to Paulus Hook, now part of Jersey City.

The second permanent settlement in Passaic County was established by Major Anthony Brockhalls and Captain Arent Schuyler. They had been driven out of New York when Governor Leisler declared them traitors to William and Mary; by the time they were able to return, Brockhalls and Schuyler had developed an interest in the Passaic County area. As a result, in 1695 they purchased 5,500 acres near Pompton and Pequannock from the Leni-Lenape. They later added 240 more acres through another purchase. This land was eventually divided into Wayne, Pompton Lakes, Ringwood, Bloomingdale, and Wanaque.

In addition to Paterson, Passaic, and Clifton, which were settled by the Ackquackanonk Patentees, other towns established by Dutch immigrants include Totowa, Little Falls, Preakness, Hackensack, Paramus, and Pompton Plains. Little Falls was typical in being settled by farmers from Ackquackanonk who purchased land as a group and then divided and farmed it. In 1711, eight Dutch farmers—Francis Post, John Sip, Harmanus Garrison, Thomas Jervanse, Christopher Stynmets, Cornelius Doremus, Peter Powlasse, and Hassel Pieterse—paid 660 pounds for the

This is an artist's conception of the Indian trading post that Hartmann Michielson established in 1678 on the island in the Passaic River. Michielson, one of the first settlers at Ackquackanonk, adopted the name Vreeland for reasons that are not clear. Courtesy, Herbert A. Fisher Collection, Julius Forstmann Library

2,800 acres that became Little Falls. They were soon joined by the Brower, Fransisco, Van Ness, and Vreeland families.

Most of the early Dutch farms were self-supporting, as a variety of crops were supplemented by foods gathered in the woods. The farmers built their houses and made most of the furniture. Some of these houses, like the Van Riper/Hopper house, are still standing. The surrounding woods provided ample lumber, and sandstone was available nearby. The livestock on a typical farm would include sheep, which provided wool that farm women wove and sewed for their clothes. Garments were generally simple and designed for work. The women made their own dyes and their own soap. Dutch family life was centered in the kitchen, particularly in the winter, as the fire used for cooking made this room the warmest in the house. It also gave off light for reading, especially of the family Bible or catechism.

The majority of early Dutch settlers were active members of the Dutch Reformed Church, and often the tiles around the fireplace were painted with pictures that were used to teach religious stories to children. Churches were a high priority in the new communities. The first Dutch Reformed Church in Ackquackanonk was established in 1690.

With the establishment of churches, ministers were required. As the number of settlers grew, so did the need for other specialists and professionals. With courts came lawyers, replacing the squire or justice of the peace who had performed routine legal functions. Soon the population was large enough to support blacksmiths, shoemakers, and eventually shopkeepers operating general stores. Many business people or professionals served more than one function. The minister, or *voorliser*, was often the schoolteacher and sometimes even the physician in addition to his clerical role. The first minister in Ackquackanonk, Guillaume Bertholf, was also the schoolteacher. There is no record of a formally trained physician in or near Ackquackanonk until fifty years after the first settlers moved in. However, Jacob Arents began in 1707 to practice folk medicine, dispensing plant and animal preparations as cures for

In addition to its vast natural resources, early settlers were drawn to Passaic County for lovely scenes such as this one, looking west from Skylands Manor in Ringwood. Courtesy, Vincent Marchese

a wide range of maladies.

The area's natural resources led to the growth of industries. One was lumbering, as both abundant timber and the river to transport logs were available. The river also provided power for mills, not only sawmills but gristmills. The first mill in the region was established by Enoch Vreeland. Another Vreeland, Dirck, ran the first brewery, used by local families to do their own distilling.

Juet's reports of copper worn by the Indians had peaked interest in Europe about the possibilities of mining in the colonies. Arent Schuyler mined copper on his property after a slave discovered the ore there by accident. The Ringwood Company began mining iron in 1742 but was not making much profit, partly due to a lack of knowledgeable ironworkers in the New World. The mercantilist laws also prohibited the manufacture of finished goods in the colonies. Iron in the form of pigs or bars had to be shipped to England and the finished goods shipped back. By 1763 the two families who made up the Ringwood Company, the Ogdens and Gouverneurs, decided to sell the mine.

Peter Hasenclever, a German living in London, saw opportunities for mining in the colonies. In 1764 he came to New Jersey and, backed by a London partnership called the American Company, purchased the Ringwood mine and put together a group of skilled German ironworkers to operate it. The Ringwood site was attractive not only because of the ore but also because of the proximity of the river and the abundance of lumber for fuel to run the ironworks. Although he went substantially over the budget provided by the American Company, Hasenclever made a success of the mine, with four furnaces and seven forges operating by 1766.

Hasenclever was a colorful character who took on the title "Baron" and had his own brass band play at dinner. His mining operations continued to expand as he opened two others in the county, one at Charlottesburg and one at Long Pond. Although it suffered from a loss of workers and absentee management, the Ringwood forge manufactured iron, made ammunition during the Revolutionary War, and provided raw material for the huge chains placed across the Hudson River to block British ships. In later years Civil War gun parts were made at this ironworks. The mine was active off and on through World War II.

Mines were also worked in Bloomingdale on the Pequannock River beginning in 1761. The Pompton ironworks, built around 1726, supplied ammunition in the French and Indian Wars as well as the Revolution.

As industry grew during the time before the Revolution, labor was often scarce. Skilled labor often had to be imported, as was the case in ironworking. The need for additional labor was frequently acute in agriculture. Workers were hard to find since land was so easy to obtain and most people interested in farming were able to have their own farms. Therefore, slaves and redemptioners were used to fill the gaps.

The Dutch had black and Indian slaves, with many farmers owning between two and twenty. Of the Northern states, New Jersey had the second largest number of slaves (after New York), mainly because of early incentives granting each new immigrant a certain number of acres for slaves he brought with him. By 1737 slaves made up 8.4 percent of the population, and nine-tenths of these had been born in the colonies. Although progress was slow, in 1804 the state passed a law requiring that the children of slaves be freed after reaching adulthood.

Also supplying labor were redemptioners, who in exchange for passage to the colonies would allow the captain of the ship to sell their services for a designated number of years. These indentured servants were frequently treated more harshly than were the slaves, since the buyer would want to receive the maximum amount of work during a limited period of time.

During the colonial period, the settlers became prosperous enough to turn their attention to government in order to protect their liberty and land holdings. Their rebellion against the payment of quitrents foreshadowed their later rebellion against the British government. When the Revolution started, the residents of the future Passaic County were prepared for their involvement in the struggle for independence.

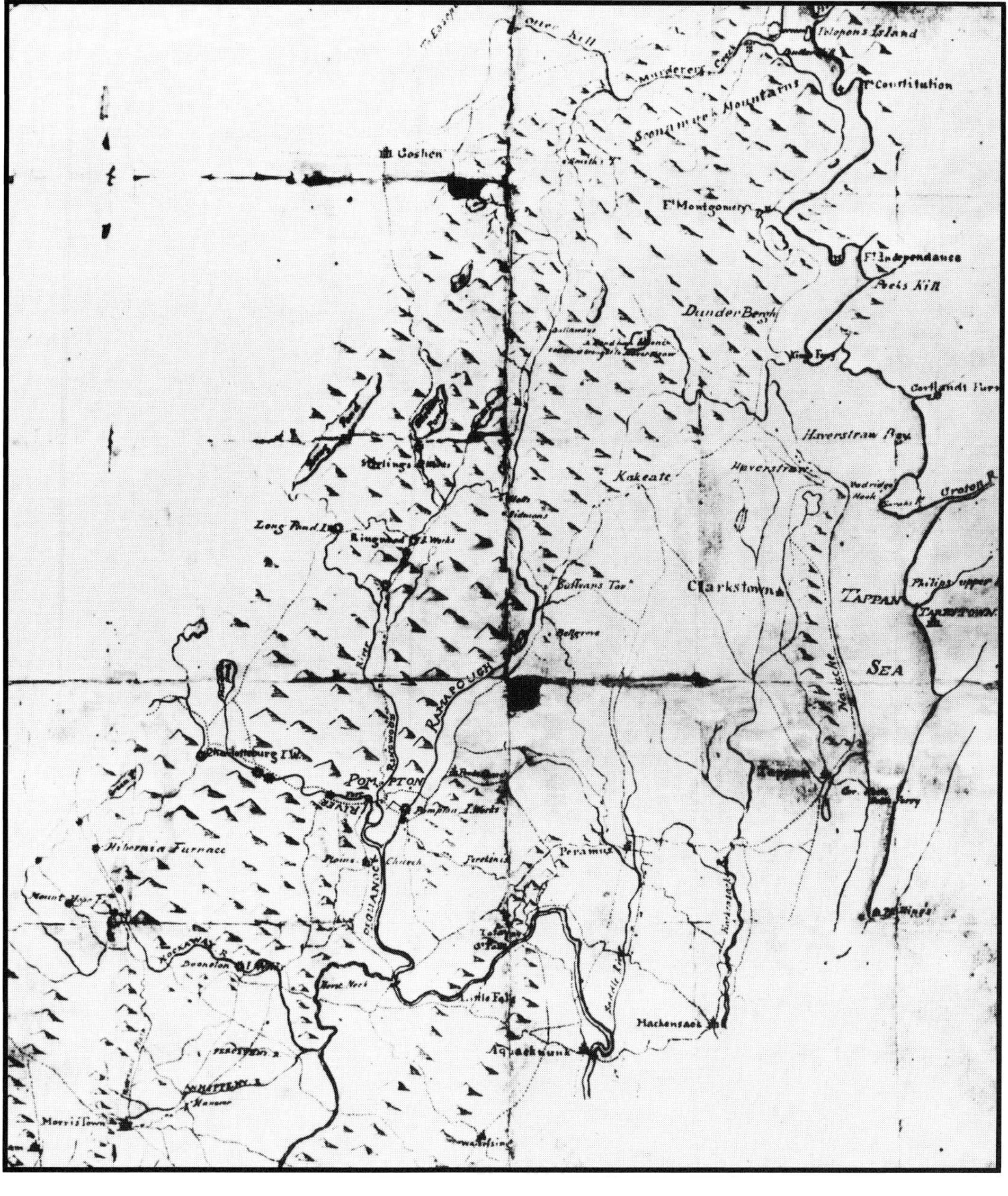

This map from the mid-1770s shows the villages, mills, and iron mines of northern New Jersey as well as southern New York. Ponds Church, the earliest settlement, is slightly lower left of center, while Totowa, Ackquackanock (Passaic), and Little Falls lie on the vertical crease near the bottom. Note the spelling of Perekinis (Preakness). Courtesy, Vincent Marchese

Chapter IV

The Revolution

While no major battles of the American Revolution were fought within the boundaries of Passaic County, no discussion of the struggle for independence would be complete if it did not include the role played by the county's people and resources.

By the time the Revolution began, New Jersey had become a prosperous colony. Most Passaic County residents were farmers who were living comfortably enough so that, initially, they were not actively involved in the rebellion. The tariffs that Parliament placed on the colonies were less onerous for this self-supporting farm population than for the residents elsewhere who were more dependent on commerce and trade.

Soon, though, Passaic County was caught up in the movement for independence. In 1765 Parliament passed an act requiring that troops be housed and fed by the province in which they were stationed. Because of New Jersey's strategic location on the route between northern and southern colonies and at an entry to the western territories, New Jersey inhabitants guessed that they were, reluctantly, about to become the hosts and benefactors of many British troops. This realization helped inspire them to join the rebel factions.

In 1774 Ackquackanonk, as one of its largest townships, took a leading role in the region's activities. When a call went out for all the colonies to set up committees of correspondence to facilitate communication, Ackquackanonk put together one of the first such committees in the state. The Ackquackanonk town committee was comprised of Michael Vreeland, Henry Garritse, Daniel Niel, Richard Ludlow, and Peter Peterse. Henry Garritse was one of nine men named to the county committee.

Another revolutionary committee—to determine who might not be on the rebels' side and generally watch over war-related activities—included the ancestors of many families well-known in this area today: Michael Vreeland, Henry Garritse, Peter Peterse, John Berry, Robert Drummond, Francis Post, Thomas Post, Daniel Niel, Richard Ludlow, Captain Abraham Godwin, John Spier, Jacob Van Riper, Lucas Wessels, Frances Van Winkle, Cornelius Van Winkle, Henry Post, Jr., Dr. Walter De Graw, John Peer, Jacob Garritse, Jacob Vreeland, Abraham Van Riper, Stephen Ryder, and Dr. Nicholas Roche. Four members of this group were selected to represent Ackquackanonk at the provincial convention: Henry Garritse, Robert Drummond, Michael Vreeland, and John Berry.

Facing page: This undated photo from the Reid Studio shows the old mill near Arcola. The mill once made blankets for Revolutionary War soldiers. Courtesy, The Paterson Museum

Robert Drummond, a member of both these select groups, tried to prevent the outbreak of war, and stayed a Tory during the war. He led a company for the British Army and retired to England after the war.

The area's most prominent supporter of the revolutionary cause was Henry Garritse, whose family owned the land now known as Garrett Mountain. In addition to serving on these committees, he was a representative to the state assembly between 1760 and 1776. George Washington was said to have visited Garritse at his home.

Although continued labor shortage made joining the military ranks difficult for many men (leaving their farms meant that necessary work went undone and their families were unprotected), Ackquackanonk contributed three militia companies to the struggle, each from a different section of the township; one from Clifton, one from Passaic, and one from the Notch (not the Great Notch of Little Falls but a smaller Notch in modern Clifton).

Ackquackanonk was favored as a campsite by American leaders. In October 1776, worried that the British forces concentrated in New York would next enter New Jersey, George Washington sent a group of surveyors to northern New Jersey to investigate possible sites for stationing the Continental troops. The Passaic River, functioning as a natural barrier, was a factor in Washington's choice of Ackquackanonk as the best spot. The location was defensible and the site of one of two existing bridges over the Passaic River. In addition, the area's game and gatherable food resources could support an army. So pleased was Washington with the location, he established his headquarters here and maintained them throughout the war under the direction of General Lord Stirling.

After this spot was chosen, Washington sent Major-General Nathanael Greene and a group of soldiers to strengthen the area's defenses. In preparation for the troops' arrival, this advance group placed cannon on the riverbank.

In the next month, Washington was forced to retreat after defeat at Fort Lee. While he and his troops were at Hackensack, he sent a letter to the Continental Congress outlining the difficulty of their location and announcing his plans to retreat across the Passaic River. On November 21, 1776, he executed his plan and marched to Ackquackanonk. After the troops had crossed, the bridge was quickly destroyed by a group led by John Post of Ackquackanonk to prevent the British from following.

Although in retreat, Washington's arrival in Ackquackanonk caused great excitement. He was greeted as a hero with cheers and speeches. There was also fear among the residents because the British were rumored to be close behind. The soldiers camped near the bridge and General Washington established headquarters at an old tavern, the Tap House on the Hill. During his stay, legend says, he met with a number of residents who offered information on local support to the army, both moral and financial.

Most of the troops departed the next day. Thomas Paine was with the army on this retreat, and while at Newark wrote his essay, "The Crisis." The differences in the kinds of difficulties the first settlers and contemporary residents faced inspired him to write the words, "These are the times that try men's souls." Confirming colonist fears, British troops followed the American forces across the Passaic four days later, at Robert's Ford. Ample food inspired this group to remain in the Clifton area for several days. On their march through the area the British troops stopped at most farms, taking what was useful to them and destroying anything they couldn't carry that might prove useful to the Continental Army.

In 1777 some American troops marched through Ackquackanonk, going from the north to the barracks at Morristown.

The Dey mansion in lower Preakness was built in 1740 by Dirck and Theunis Dey. Theunis was a colonel in the Revolution. Courtesy, Passaic County Historical Society

Unfortunately, these desperate troops, lacking food and clothing, further contributed to the pillaging that the residents along this route had already suffered.

In the same year, a raid by British General Henry Clinton led to the establishment of a signal system so that lookouts could warn residents of enemy approaches. As the system, which involved firing guns in the daytime and lighting fires at night to signal danger, was not foolproof, a more permanent guard was established at Ackquackanonk.

While staying here Washington and his troops used a hill near the Great Notch as a lookout. Lawrence A. Trumbull, in *History of Industrial Paterson,* wrote that Washington saw a British party leaving Elizabeth from this point and was able to send troops in time to stop the raiders.

One of the few skirmishes to occur in Passaic arose when an Ackquackanonk farmer, John Wanshair, tried to protect his property from the British troops. Some of Wanshair's neighbors came to his aid, but they were ridiculously outnumbered and the British made off with livestock and possessions. A second encounter took place in Ackquackanonk after the Battle of Monmouth, but the British crossed the bridge and escaped before the skirmish with local militiamen could escalate to battle proportions.

In June of 1778 a division of the Continental Army was led through Ackquackanonk by General Israel Putnam on the way to the Hudson River and again in December as it proceeded to Middlebrook.

The army was encamped in the region again in 1780. This time, Washington stayed at the Dey home, built in the Preakness section of Wayne by Dirck and his son Theunis Dey in the 1740s. Theunis Dey served as a freeholder in Bergen County and then as a state assemblyman. When the Revolution began he joined the militia and became a colonel. In his role as head of the Bergen county militia, he became a close friend of Washington. During the time the Dey mansion served as his headquarters, Washington completed a great deal of correspondence, met with members of Congress and directed an attack on Bull's Ferry, a British-occupied blockhouse. Many of that time's well known figures—Lafayette, Anthony

Wayne, Lord Stiring, and even Benedict Arnold—visited Washington at the Dey home.

The Dey mansion had a series of owners between the time the Dey family sold it in 1802 and the present owners, the Passaic County Park Commission, took possession in 1930. In 1929 the state legislature had authorized funds for restoration of the home but due to the Depression the funds were never made available and the property was eventually sold to the park commission. Some restoration of this Georgian home was done in 1933 by the Civil Works Administration.

Washington left the Dey home in July of 1780, taking his army to Paramus. He returned in October, shaken by the news of Benedict Arnold's treason, and feeling that this area was less accessible to the British than was the Hudson River Valley, where the troops had most recently been stationed. Washington left the Dey mansion for the second time in November 1780. Some of the soldiers left this area for Morristown; some remained at Pompton. NP–Rifle troops were located here for a time, encamped on what it is known today as, "Rifle Camp Road." This unit turned back a British calvary detachment that tried to cross American lines, allegedly to kidnap General Washington.

In 1781 there was mutiny among the soldiers, who were then stationed at Pompton. One group was about to mutiny against the harsh conditions and lack of pay. On hearing reports of this crisis Washington was alarmed and decided drastic action was necessary. He sent additional American troops to Pompton who surrounded the camp, then court-martialed and executed two of the mutiny's leaders. There were no further reports of attempted mutiny by this group.

Washington passed through Ackquackanonk again in 1782. Legend says that his wife, Martha, was with him on this trip

Troops passing through Paterson during the American Revolution were no doubt awed by the beauty and power of the Great Falls, shown in this 1880s Harper's Weekly lithograph. Courtesy, Vincent Marchese

During the American Revolution, George Washington used the Dey Mansion, shown as it appears today, as his headquarters. Courtesy, Vincent Marchese

According to legend, Alexander Hamilton had the original idea for the establishment of Paterson while visiting the Great Falls with George Washington. His statue, dedicated by former President Gerald Ford. now overlooks the waterway. Courtesy, The Paterson Museum

and that they stopped at the Schuyler house in Pompton.

During the Revolution, the Ringwood ironworks were still active under the direction of Robert Erskine, Washington's surveyor-general and mapmaker. Erskine also supervised the production of the bulk of the Continental Army's cannon and ammunition. During the course of the Revolution the works were completely devoted to manufacturing goods needed for the war. As many as 600 men were employed in the mine and forge at this time, some of whom doubled as soldiers since iron manufacturing had affected the manpower shortage. Military personnel were needed not merely as workers but also for protection; an iron manufacturing plant was a likely target for British raids.

The Bloomingdale furnace was probably not active during the Revolution, but the Pompton ironworks, although hampered by a lack of manpower, produced ammunition. The cannonballs made at Pompton were said to have been transported by means of a less-traveled road (which is now Route 202) to lessen the possibility of British raids. This route, the legendary Cannonball Road, now just a small overgrown trail, ran from Pompton to the Hudson.

Passaic County offered campsites with access to game and forageable food many times during the Revolution, providing a haven for George Washington, and serving as a point of control of the paths both armies would travel. Passaic County's iron resources and smelting facilities helped supply the Continental Army with guns and ammunition. Indeed, the lives of the citizens of Passaic County were significantly changed by the war. Their future and that of their children were soon to be changed even more appreciably by one of the men their struggle for independence had fortuitously brought to the falls—Alexander Hamilton.

Chapter V

The Arrival and Survival of Industry

Winning the American Revolution brought political independence, but the colonies would not be completely free until economic autonomy was also won. Before the war, most goods not made in the home were imported from England. The new nation would have to develop its own manufacturing capability to end economic dependence on the British. In 1776, achieving this goal seemed a long way off.

As early as 1700 Ackquackanonk was already a production and distribution center for lumber and building supplies and Enoch Vreeland and Abraham Zabriskie among others, had established mills in the region.

Drawn by abundant prospects for trading, and easy water transportation, New Yorker Stephen Bassett established one of New Jersey's first tanneries in 1735 in Acquackanonk.

By the turn of the century several forges and furnaces were active in the northern part of the county; shoes, glassware, lumber, and cloth were manufactured in small quantities; and many mills, both saw and grist, were operating. John Bradbury was one of those who ran a gristmill. Built in 1698 and later converted into a paper mill, Bradbury's building became home to the company publishing the *Ladies' Home Journal*.

Despite these beginnings, all the colonists' needs were not being met. After the Revolutionary War, the new nation suffered an economic depression. Fabric was in heavy demand after England was eliminated as a supply source, and most cloth produced in the colonies was made at home. Given this modest beginning, it is not surprising that John Adams wrote to Benjamin Franklin in 1780, predicting, "America will not make manufactures enough for her own consumption these thousand years."

Adams failed to take into consideration the skill and determination of manufacturing's strong advocate, Alexander Hamilton. While a student at Columbia University, then King's College, Hamilton had spoken on the need for domestic manufacturing of essential products. In 1777 he became George Washington's aide-de-camp, who appointed him secretary of the treasury in 1789. In this position Hamilton's responsibilities included developing the manufacturing capability necessary for the nation's survival. Cognizant of one of the major obstacles to industrial development—the lack of power to run the factories—he saw this water power as the

Facing page: This elaborate arch at Ellison and Main streets greeted visitors to the centennial celebration of 1892. The arch reads, "By Industry We Thrive." Courtesy, The Paterson Museum

answer to the nation's first energy crisis.

In 1791 Hamilton presented his "Report on Manufactures" to Congress and emphasized the need to produce basics such as cotton, thread, and paper in America. He envisioned the establishment of a centralized manufacturing site and convinced the New Jersey legislature to grant a charter empowering a committee to create an industrial center. So, in November 1791, the "Society for Establishing Useful Manufactures" (SUM) was established and thirteen directors were chosen: William Duer, John Dewhurst, Benjamin Walker, Nicholas Low, Royal Flint, Elias Boudinot, John Bayard, John Neilson, Archibald Mercer, Thomas Lowering, George Lewis, More Furman, and Alexander McComb.

Since the charter did not specify a location for the manufacturing center, the directors' first task was to choose a site. Many towns in New Jersey, New York, and Pennsylvania submitted development proposals, including Ackquackanonk, which noted that "the natural lay of the land afforded hundreds of excellent mill sites." Little Falls also submitted a proposal, but ultimately, as Hamilton hoped, the SUM chose the area near the Great Falls.

The site had a number of advantages. The primary one was the availability of water power to run the mills. Also, both wood and iron ore could be found locally, and sandstone could be quarried nearby for building. In addition, the Passaic River provided easy transportation to New York City.

Committee officials announced their choice in May 1791, and declared the city name to be "Paterson," after the governor, William Paterson, who had approved the charter. Some had suggested the town be named "Hamilton," but Hamilton, aware of his political unpopularity, insisted another choice be made.

The New Jersey charter granted the SUM control of the waterways, exemption from all taxes for ten years and all but state taxes after that time. Through its economic control the Society seemed to govern the city but never established a real government. For forty years, until the citizens received a revised charter from the legislature in 1831, Paterson had no govern-

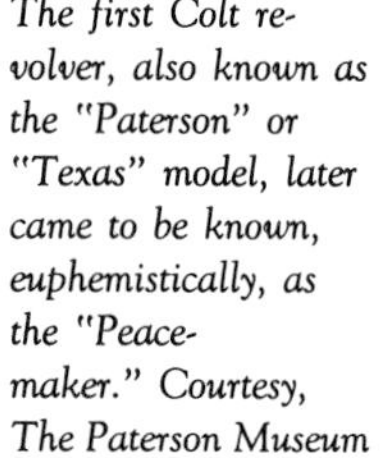

The first Colt revolver, also known as the "Paterson" or "Texas" model, later came to be known, euphemistically, as the "Peacemaker." Courtesy, The Paterson Museum

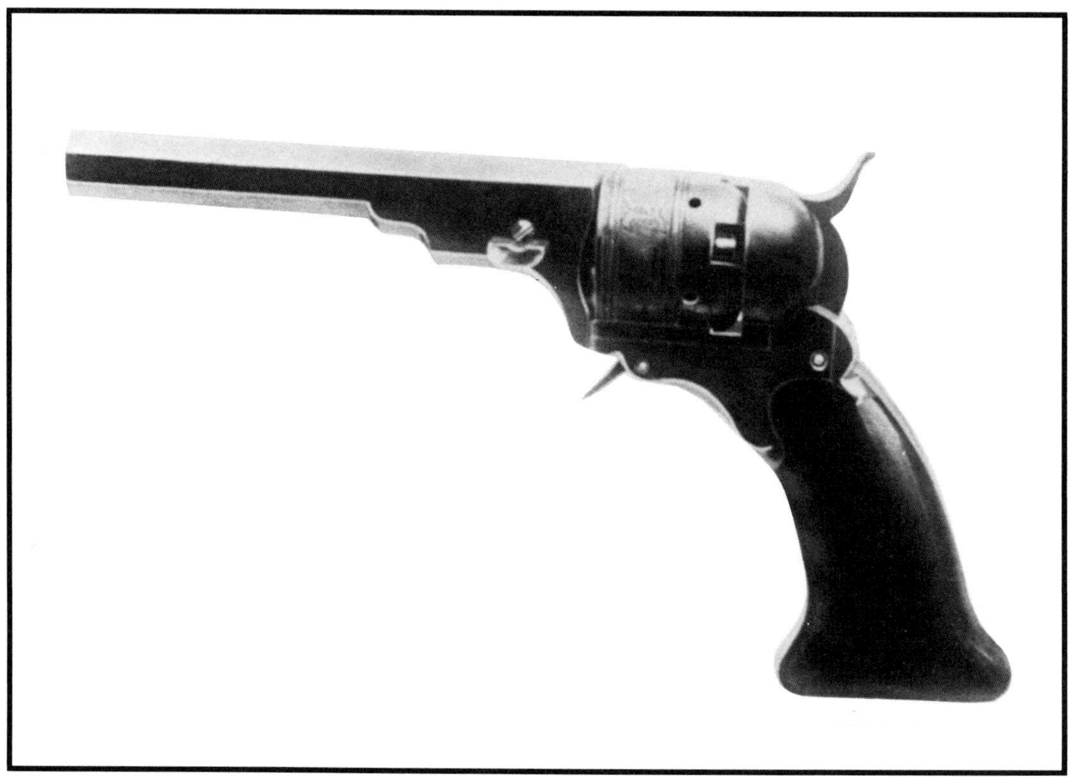

ment. Paterson shares with Washington, D.C., the honor of being the first two planned cities in the nation, and neither began with their own municipal governments. The Society first purchased 700 acres plus the river beds above and below the falls. For this, it paid $8,230, or about twelve dollars per acre, a bargain even in 1791. Many families profited from the land purchases, such as the Van Houten, Van Blarcom, Post, Blain, Godwin, Blatchley, Willis, and Van Gieson families.

Pierre L'Enfant, a friend of Hamilton's, was initially retained to design Paterson. His proposals were too ambitious and impractical for the Society, though, and well beyond its limited budget.

Peter Colt, then secretary of the treasury in Connecticut, replaced L'Enfant. He made the SUM guarantee the city's success before he moved his family. The first of many Colts who would influence the development of Paterson, Peter was one of the owners of the only factory then making cloth in the new nation. One of his sons, John, would firmly establish the cotton industry by developing a process for making cotton duck on a loom; another son, Roswell, was instrumental in rejuvenating the SUM in 1814. Morgan Colt, Roswell's son, followed his father as governor of the SUM. From another branch of the family came Samuel Colt, who invented the Colt revolver. And finally, Christoper Colt was the first person to bring silk machinery into Paterson, beginning one of the city's major industries. It was also Peter's sister, Sarah who began the first Sunday school in New Jersey in 1794.

John Colt's plans seemed more realistic to the Society. He oversaw the building of the first mill in Paterson, which was completed in 1793. Ironically, this mill's wheel was not turned by water power generated by the Passaic River, but by an ox on a treadmill, earning it the name "Bull Mill." The ox was replaced by water power

The mills of lower Passaic County attracted workers from dozens of countries in the late 1800s. Most were fiercely proud of their ethnic heritages, such as this Scotsman dressed in full clan regalia in a photo from the 1880s. Courtesy, Passaic County Historical Society

the following year. This was the second successful attempt at spinning cotton by machinery in the country, the first being at Beverly, Rhode Island, in 1790. In the 1820s this original mill was replaced by another that burned in 1848. The Hamil Mill was built on the same site in 1873 and housed Robert Hamil and James Booth's silk business until 1903. The Hamil Mill is among those still standing that have been recently renovated.

Colt's design of the raceways included stone channels used to carry water from the river to the mill wheels. They were built from sandstone quarried nearby. Colt's plan called for a series of three raceways, each twenty-two feet higher than the next so that the same water could provide equal power for the mills on different levels. The last raceway to be completed, the uppermost one, was finished in 1828. These raceways were among the first engineering projects in the country to involve water power. Enough water was diverted from the river to the raceways that during dry periods only a small stream of water ran over the falls.

Farmers balked at the idea of moving their children off the farms and into factories and the Society chose not to use slave labor in the mills. Consequently, the development plan called for recruiting workers from New York City and Europe. European workers were cheaper and had skills that Americans lacked. On the other hand, Paterson lacked housing and a municipal infrastructure. The houses provided for mill workers and their families were eighteen feet by twenty-four feet. The Society appropriated $170 to build each house, which could then be rented for $12.50 per year, or purchased for $250, to be paid within twenty years. If a worker wished to build, he could purchase one-quarter of an acre for eighty-eight dollars.

The SUM suffered many setbacks. The stock market plummeted in 1792. One of the directors, sent to England with $50,000 to buy materials and machine parts, disappeared with the funds. Stockholders would not pay their installments and the amount raised through a lottery was reduced drastically, from original expectations of $40,000 to $6,600. By 1797, the Society, without rental income from a larger group of factories was unable to provide the support required by a small group of industries and was forced to suspend operations. Portions of the recently opened cotton mill were rented to small operators and the directors met infrequently. When these first ventures failed Paterson became a ghost town. Although the population had reached 500 when the mill was working, it had dropped to a little more than forty by 1797. The Colt family gained control of the SUM corporation by purchasing its shares.

Sparked by the inventor of a continuous roll paper manufacturing process, Charles Kinsey, industry slowly began to return to Paterson in the early nineteenth century. Kinsey's company, Kinsey, Crane and Fairchild, began operations in Paterson in 1804.

Kinsey hit upon the continuous roll process for paper while watching cotton being carded onto thin webs. He patented his new process in 1807 and was entirely unaware that Louis Robet had patented the same process in France ten years earlier (but had never used it as a production process). The real irony of Kinsey's process was that it worked so well, his partners, with greater profits in mind, stopped using it for paper and switched to cotton, to the enormous displeasure of the bemused Kinsey. Other enterprises soon followed.

John Clark, Paterson's first machinist, also established himself during this period. Clark made machinery for spinning mills and eventually opened a much needed machinist training school, and one of Peter Colt's sons, John, opened a cotton mill, but Paterson was still far from the bustling center it would later become.

The War of 1812 helped Paterson's economy by creating a need for cloth for soldiers' uniforms. But when the war ended, a brief but severe depression followed. Philemon Dickerson, a prominent Paterson citizen, described the emptiness this depression brought on in a lecture to the Paterson Educational Association many years later: "for in 1816 I have walked in the middle of a clear day in Main Street from the corner of Congress Street to the river, without meeting a single human being. That was indeed a gloomy time, and this almost a deserted village."

Despite hopeful signs, in 1814 the SUM was close to dissolution; its affairs were almost hopelessly complicated and its stock almost worthless. But at a meeting in April of that year, the directors determined to aggressively pursue the reestablishment of industry. At this point, the Colt family held 1,991 of the Society's 2,620 shares of stock. Led by Roswell Colt, who controlled the SUM for forty years until his death in 1856, the rejuvenation effort succeeded with growth continuing well into the 1830s, when it was temporarily interrupted in 1837 by a nationwide depression. As it had done earlier, Paterson bounced back from this setback. Protective tariffs instituted in 1816 helped this growth, as did the arrival of two new industries: locomotive manufacturing and silk production.

While these two industries were just beginning, cotton was growing at a great rate. In 1814, there were eleven working cotton mills using up 1.5 million pounds of raw cotton per year, and by 1832 there were twenty mills using 5,860,272 pounds of raw cotton annually.

John Colt helped boost the cotton industry in 1822 when he made the first cotton duck that did not require dressing to protect against mildew. Colt's material was particularly well suited for sails as it withstood moisture well. Demand for this product led Colt to develop a process for manufacturing this fabric on a power-loom in 1824. By the 1830s all the sails used by the US Navy were being made in Paterson. Even the yacht, *America*, used Colt sails when she won the America's Cup race in 1851.

Despite the gradual eclipse of cotton as Paterson's dominant product, it was an active industry through the end of the nineteenth century. Firms such as the R.H. Adams Company and the Enterprise Manufacturing Company continued to manufacture cotton goods for some time. In 1872 S. Holt and Sons developed Turkish towels—terry cloth—and later Robert Holt and J. Miller manufactured them. Philip Schott made cotton counterpanes and George and Alexander McLean produced mosquito netting and buckram. Buckram was an important material used as the backing on rugs and for making sacks. By 1881 raw cotton production in Paterson increased to 3,850,000 pounds. It was processed by approximately 950 employees. There were also advances in cotton bleaching and dyeing operations.

The SUM sponsored bleaching cotton by hand in 1794, and put up a building for cotton bleaching in 1836. Bleaching and dyeing became significant parts of Paterson's cotton industry with many mills involved, including the Victory Mill, run by John Murphy, and the Franklin, Mallory, and Passaic Mills, operated by the Franklin Manufacturing Company.

The interdependence of Paterson's industry is illustrated by the lateral movement of workers in seemingly different industries. The machinery required to produce cotton first attracted to the area machinists and metal workers who would go on to build locomotive engines. Similarly, when the silk industry took hold, skills and equipment utilized in cotton production were easily transferable.

Attempts at American silk production were encouraged by James I in Virginia as early as 1608. Experiments in England had not been successful and he looked to the colonies as a more suitable environment for raising silkworms and producing raw silk. As English law prohibited colonists from producing finished goods from raw products, this arrangement had the added benefit of providing British manufacturers a supply of raw materials while ensuring dependence on England for their products. Eventually some raw silk was produced, but not enough to call this endeavor a success.

In the 1830s the American government also attempted to promote raw silk production by encouraging cultivation of mulberry trees and offering fifteen cents per pound for silkworm cocoons. Silkworms must eat mulberry leaves to thrive and produce silk. The government's offer and the number of private firms purchasing silkworms led to a surge of interest and soon cultivating mulberry trees was a very popular venture. Unfortunately, silkworms also need a very mild climate to survive and soon large numbers of people who had hoped to make their fortunes producing raw silk became the owners of fairly useless mulberry trees.

Since attempts at producing raw silk in this country failed, manufacturers of silk goods switched to importing the raw material from the Orient and the Mediterranean. Combined with the recruitment of foreign silk industry professionals, there was some interest in manufacturing.

Christopher Colt was responsible for bringing the first silk making machinery into Paterson, around 1838. Colt established his business in a section of the Gun Mill but only a little fabric was manufactured and the business closed shortly after it had been established.

As Colt was experimenting with the new industry, a young man named John Ryle was working in a Northhampton, Massachusetts, fabric mill and by chance encountered a traveler, George Murray, whose own silk business had been destroyed by fire. Murray believed in silk as a viable venture and encouraged Ryle to try it. Shortly thereafter Ryle moved to New York City and established a silk importing business. In New York, Murray again met Ryle by chance and told him of Christopher Colt's vacated facilities. In 1840 Murray purchased Colt's business and employed Ryle to run it.

In 1843 Murray and Ryle became partners, forming a relationship which lasted until 1846 when Murray retired. Eventually the business grew and Ryle purchased the Gun Mill, renting out the space he did not require for his own operation. He built two more structures near the original Gun Mill and by 1850 employed more than 500 workers. John Ryle established the "Silk City" of Paterson.

John C. Benson also entered the Paterson silk industry in about 1850, and conducted operations in the Beaver Mill until 1860 or 1861. Benson was soon followed by John Birchenough, James Whitehall, and partners Robert Hamil and James Booth, who together operated the Hamil Mill. This group was initially responsible for escalating Paterson's growing fame as "Silk City."

Ryle's contributions in particular were marked by a series of awards. He received recognition for being the first person to make sewing silk in the United States, the first to put silk on a spool, and as the maker of the first silk American flag, which flew over the Crystal Palace at the New York World's Fair in 1852.

Ryle later built the Murray Mill. He celebrated the opening of this mill by throwing a large sit-down dinner party in the mill to which all 500 employees were invited. In 1857 the firm was hard hit by a national depression, however, having extended large amounts of credit that became uncollectable. Ryle, dissolved his own company and joined with his nephew, William Ryle, to form a new firm. When the Murray Mill burned in 1869, the second company was ruined for lack of fire in-

As laborers had their organizations, so did management. These silk mill superintendents were photographed in the late 1870s or early 1880s. Courtesy, Passaic County Historical Society

This social worker visits a silk worker's family on an unknown street in lower Passaic County. Courtesy, The Paterson Museum

surance. Not easily discouraged, Ryle set about raising new capital to form the Ryle Silk Manufacturing Company. When this firm went broke in 1872, Ryle established John Ryle and Sons, which later merged with the Pioneer Silk Company.

As the silk industry's most famous and powerful proponent, Ryle spent much of 1864 in Washington, D.C., lobbying for repeal of a tariff on imported raw materials. He found the government more preoccupied with the Civil War, and his persistence led to success: the tariff was removed and Paterson manufacturers were put into competition with foreign firms.

Thomas N. Dale was another entrepreneur who benefited greatly from Paterson's fabric industry. Like many others, Dale began with virtually no money, but worked and traded his way to success as president of a company supplying goods other than fabric to tailors. Dale became interested in the silk industry, took on several partners, and constructed the huge Dale Mill in Paterson. Apparently a bit overambitious, he destroyed his fortune with debts incurred in setting up the business and building the mill. Paterson entrepreneurs like Ryle and Dale never believed in half-measures, which was the secret of their successes—and stunning reverses.

Catholina Lambert was one of Paterson's best known "Silk Barons." Like Ryle, Lambert had worked in mills in England before coming to the United States in 1851. Initially employed by Tilt and Dexter, a Boston firm, Lambert was taken on as a clerk and eventually became a partner. The company's products were silk decorations, and trimmings used for a wide variety of purposes including military uniforms, household decorations, and carriages and trimmings for undertakers.

Lambert made several trips to Paterson and became convinced that this city would be a better location for the firm. Dexter, Lambert and Company moved to its new

Quackenbush & Son Hardware Store, located at 123-125 Main Street, was photographed on April 20, 1897. Leaning at the left of the entrance is John D. Quackenbush; in the doorway, Harry Sturr; standing with his hands on hips is Peter C. Quackenbush; at the right of the door with his hands clasped is David P. Quackenbush; next to him is John Hagerdorn, and at right is the store clerk, Joe. Courtesy, Passaic County Historical Society

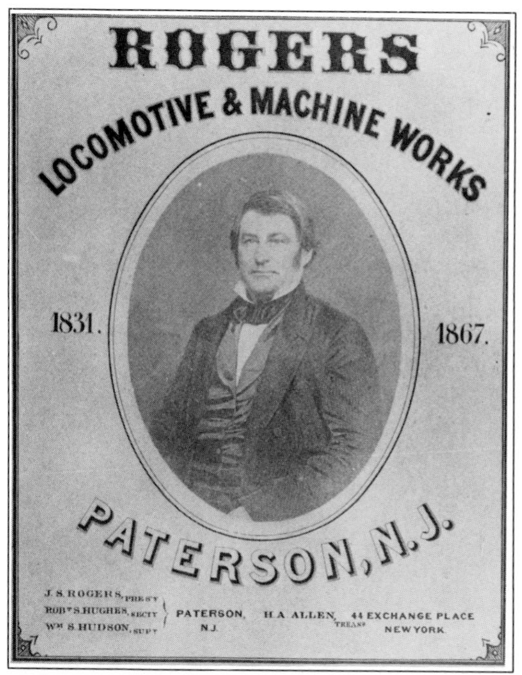

Above: The Rogers Locomotive Works were an early mainstay of Passaic County's economy. Rogers was second in size only to the Baldwin Works in Philadelphia. Rogers' locomotives and rolling stock saw service around the world. Courtesy, The Paterson Museum

Right: These men paused for a photo in the planning department of Rogers' Works in August of 1897. Courtesy, The Paterson Museum

location on Straight Street in 1866. By 1882 Dexter, Lambert had facilities in both Paterson and Pennsylvania, employed approximately 1,000 workers and was doing more than one million dollars worth of business annually.

As he became wealthy, Lambert wanted to build a residence rivalling those he had seen as a child in England, and so constructed Belle Vista Castle on Garrett Mountain. Dexter, Lambert encountered the same problems experienced by other silk firms in the early 1900s, however, and Lambert was forced to sell much of an extensive art collection he had gathered at the castle. The collection, valued at between 1.5 and two million dollars, brought in but

Above: The Lathe shop at Rogers Locomotive and Machine Works was photographed in 1897. Electricity had only recently replaced steam power to run the belts, resulting in more power and productivity. Courtesy, The Paterson Museum

Left: The first floor of a Paterson machine shop, possibly Rogers', was photographed in 1897. Courtesy, The Paterson Museum

In the pattern shop at Rogers Works, templates were cut to mold and guide every element, no matter how small, in Rogers' many machine parts and locomotives. Courtesy, The Paterson Museum

The drawing department at Rogers Works was hardly the comfortable designer's office or architect's loft of today. Yet, from such offices came the blueprints for America's eventual lead in world industrial production. Courtesy, The Paterson Museum

one-third of that amount through an auction; however, it was enough to get Lambert out of debt.

When Lambert died in 1923 Belle Vista Castle, now most often referred to as Lambert's Castle, was sold to the City of Paterson and later to the Passaic County Park Commission, which along with the Passaic County Historical Society has its offices there.

While the English silk industry suffered a severe decline in 1860, Paterson's silk industry grew. Workers, managers, and former business owners all emigrated to Paterson, which benefited from their skills and experience. The industry continued to grow and between 1872 and 1881 the annual total output of silk products grew from more than $9.5 million to almost $16,250,000. By 1881 there were 121 firms in Paterson involved in silk production, either in manufacturing, dyeing, or making supplies and equipment needed by the silk industry.

Parallel to the rise of the silk industry was machine tooling manufacturing. Although George Parkinson was the first to build machinery in Paterson, John Clark, who came to Paterson from Scotland, was largely responsible for launching machine manufacturing as an industry. The earliest machines were constructed mostly from wood, with some parts in iron that was sometimes smelted, beaten, and forged by the mines and forges of Ringwood, Pompton, and Charolottsburg in northern Passaic County.

The Rogers, Ketchum and Grosvenor Iron and Brass Foundry was photographed between 1857 and 1860. Train wheels, cannon caissons, and cannon flank workers are in the yard. Courtesy, Passaic County Historical Society

From the nascent mechanical industry came entrepreneurs such as Thomas Rogers, who founded an industry soon to overshadow the parts manufacturing and metal working businesses. Born in Connecticut, Rogers came to Paterson in 1812 when he was about twenty years old. John Clark employed him as a carpenter and when Clark retired, his son took on Rogers as a partner. Later, Rogers left Clark with two new partners, Morris Ketchum and Joseph Grosvenor. Their firm was engaged in making axles, wheels, and parts for railroad bridges.

Rogers' imagination was captivated in 1835 when he re-assembled a locomotive, the *MacNeil,* shipped to the United States in pieces from England. Convinced that he could do at least as well at building his own locomotive, he constructed his first locomotive engine, the *Sandusky,* and gave the industry its start in Paterson. The *Sandusky* was shipped to Ohio in 1837, which forced the Ohio state legislature to standardize the track width in the state at four feet, ten inches, to accommodate the engine's wheels. This was a necessity because the *Sandusky* was used to help lay most of the state's tracks.

The speed with which Rogers, Ketchum, and Grosvenor turned out locomotives increased, and although the factory only manufactured one in 1837, it finished seven the following year and by 1854 was turning out 103 in one year. Rogers added new inventions to his locomotives, including the steam whistle, and painted each one with bright paint and decoration.

Soon, other companies were established to meet the increasing demand for locomotives. William Swinburne, who had assisted Rogers in building the *Sandusky,* joined with Samuel Smith to found Swinburne, Smith and Company, which in 1848 became the second company in Paterson to be engaged in this business. After Swinburne left the company in 1852, the firm became the New Jersey Locomotive Company, and then was purchased in 1865 by Oliver D.F. Grant and his son, D.B. Grant, and renamed the Grant Locomotive Works. These works built the locomotive *America,* exhibited at the Paris Exposition in 1867. Because of its detailing, including silver mountings and native woods, the engine was described by a contemporary writer as a "veritable poem in iron and steel and silver." Between its founding and the start of the Civil War, the Grant Works produced 225 engines.

The founders and guiding forces in the locomotive industry shared a determination with those in the silk industry. John Cooke was one who began working in the Rogers, Ketchum and Grosvenor plant, where his father worked. His work and study were rewarded in 1852 when he was made a partner at Danforth, becoming president of the Danforth Works when Danforth retired. The firm was reorganized as Danforth, Cooke and Company and in March 1853 it completed its first engine. By 1859 the firm was turning out thirty-five locomotives a year. Grant was also doing a profitable business and between 1860 and 1881 turned out almost 1,300 engines, with production per year ranging from ten in 1875 to 131 in 1873. When the Civil War began, Paterson and Philadelphia were together manufacturing 75 percent of America's locomotives, as well as supplying

The Danforth and Cooke Company was a major locomotive manufacturer in Paterson in the mid-nineteenth century. The three principals of the company posed with an elaborate 2-2-4 engine in about 1861. From left to right are John Cooke, Charles Danforth, and Joseph Dougherty. Courtesy, Passaic County Historical Society

Workers at the Danforth and Cooke Locomotive and Machine Company were photographed around 1890. From left to right are William Forbs, Frank Lovell, Adolph Wold, P. King, William Cambell, Charles D. Cooke, and James Binney. Courtesy, Passaic County Historical Society

engines to other countries.

Rogers, Ketchum and Grosvenor was prosperous, too. A fire in 1879 destroyed the works but it was soon rebuilt. The economic panic of 1873 brought the firm to a low of fifty employees building fourteen engines in 1877, but only four years later, 1,800 were employed and 240 locomotives were produced.

A new source of demand for locomotives was presented by the building of the Panama Canal with 144 Paterson-built locomotives employed in the canal's construction of which 100 were Cooke *Mogul* engines. One of the engines ordered by the Canal Commission was the 299 (the locomotives had numbers rather than names). The 299 continued active service until 1953 when it was put on display in the Canal Zone. In 1979, Paterson Mayor Lawrence F. Kramer negotiated the return of the 299 to Paterson. The locomotive was pulled into Paterson in June of 1979 and now stands outside The Paterson Museum housed in the old Rogers' Works.

Factories and mills also were turning out a variety of other products such as woolens, paper, shirts, soap, candles, and chemicals. Paterson became a center for engraving, marble cutting, and preserving processes, and brewing developed into a significant industry with eight breweries turning out approximately 100,000 barrels annually.

Endeavors in other lines of manufacturing were being pursued as well. Samuel Colt, distantly related to Peter Colt, designed the first models of his famed revolver in the structure that came to be known as the Gun Mill. Before building the Gun Mill, Colt had operated a rolling mill and nail manufacturing plant on the site. Initially, Colt had no luck in interesting anyone in

The factories of Paterson are shown on a quiet winter morning in the 1920s. City Hall and the public school are visible to the right of center in the background. Courtesy, The Paterson Museum

These workers are shown loading finished pipe from the East Jersey Pipe Company onto a Boston & Maine Railroad flat car, between 1910-1920. At the time, the Paterson and Passaic County area was the industrial hub of New Jersey. Courtesy, Passaic County Historical Society

his guns, in spite of extensive promotional efforts. A demonstration at West Point failed to convince the United States Army of their value. Discouraged, Colt closed up his Paterson operation and moved to Hartford, Connecticut, where he shared Eli Whitney's facilities. The Colt Revolver later became a success when used by the Texas Rangers and in the Mexican-American War.

The power of water was recognized in other parts of the county. Envisioning the possibilities of water power, two Ackquackanonk residents, John S. Van Winkle and Brant Van Blarcom, built a raceway on the Passaic River at Ackquackanonk. These two then sold their land and water rights to Jacob Van Winkle who anticipated even greater potential but needed funds to complete the construction required to harness this energy. In 1832 he joined Jacob M. Ryerson, Peter M. Ryerson, Russell Stebbins, A.R. Thompson, and William Chase to form the Dundee Manufacturing Company. The company was authorized to raise $150,000 for constructing facilities to manufacture iron, cotton, wool, and other practical articles.

The Dundee Manufacturing Company, like the SUM, had its problems. The sawmills had quickly used all the lumber in the area and only enough grain was brought

While the majority of the county's citizens lived plain, hard-working lives during the Industrial Revolution, the business magnates lived in ease and luxury. Courtesy, The Paterson Museum

A poor childhood in Passaic at the turn of the century offered little hope of advancement. Streets in the poorer quarters were drab and offered little in the way of diversion or education. Courtesy, The Paterson Museum

in to keep one gristmill busy. The mills were a mile away from navigable river waters, making transportation of products difficult. Also, the Dundee Manufacturing Company was hit by the 1837 depression before it had a chance to become firmly established.

A Trenton resident, Edward J.C. Atterbury, suggested building a larger dam to supply more power, and lengthening the navigable part of the river. The Dundee Manufacturing Company then gained permission to go ahead with the building of a canal. Atterbury took over as president and under his direction a twenty-two-foot dam and system of locks on a canal were built. The company hoped to raise revenue by charging boats for passage through the locks. Disappointingly, there wasn't demand for transport on this part of the river and only one boat passed through the locks. Eventually the company was put up for sale. Atterbury purchased it and reorganized as the Dundee Water Power and Land Company. The company operated five mills along the river and by 1892 had worked off its debts.

Other spots along the path of the Passaic River were locations for industry. In 1846, Robert Beattie relocated to Little Falls from New York City and built a carpet mill at the falls. The endeavor was a success and the

This scene looks south on Main Street from Broadway in the late 1860s or early 1870s. Courtesy, The Paterson Museum

In an undated photo, this delivery wagon for the Consumer's Baking Company was decked out for either a Fourth of July parade or for the Centennial of 1892. Courtesy, Passaic County Historical Society

Beattie Rug Company continued to grow and expand from the 1850s until the 1970s.

Other mills were added to the already existing sawmills and gristmills in the vicinity of Little Falls, including one established by George Jackson in 1850 that manufactured felt.

While most industries recovered and prospered after the nationwide depression in 1857 and the Civil War, banking did not fare as well. Only one bank, the Passaic City Bank, survived the collapses that led an effort to improve the banking system. In fact, despite pressing need, attempts to establish banks were largely unsuccessful until the late 1800s. Various banks had come and gone in the county but none had lasted any length of time. The most pressing need was in the county's only real city, Paterson, where the majority of the county's residents lived. Area residents depended on New York City banks for loans. The Paterson Bank, incorporated in 1815, was the city's first. It failed in 1829 but was reorganized in 1834, only to be destroyed in the 1837 depression. In 1864 a charter was granted for the organization of the First National Bank in Paterson. The bank's primary mover, George Stimson, became ill, and four months after receiving the charter the bank was liquidated before it had opened. John Brown assumed the task of reorganizing the bank, raised the necessary capital, and opened it for business in September 1864. The bank moved several times as it grew and was sound enough to survive the panic of 1873. Garret A. Hobart who became vice president under President William McKinley, served on First National's Board of Directors.

In 1886 the Passaic National Bank, the first to be successful, opened in Passaic. This was followed by the Passaic Trust and Safe Deposit Company and the Passaic National Bank and Trust Company, which was a merger of Passaic's first two banks. The People's Bank and Trust Company, the Hobart Trust Company, the Merchant's Bank of Passaic, and the City Trust Company of Passaic survived and prospered. A number of mortgage companies and building and loan associations sprang up as well.

It must be said that banking in Passaic County has been an active field in this century. When Franklin Roosevelt declared a "Bank Holiday" in 1933 to re-evaluate the banks, Paterson bankers combined their cash, providing enough of a bank to allow business to continue, an action that received national attention. Several innovations were brought about by local banks. Passaic National was a leader in installment loans and personal checking. In the 1920s Clifton National initiated "Ladies' Loans." A precursor to equal credit opportunity movements, Clifton National allowed a woman to take out a loan without her husband's knowledge or approval—a fairly radical concept for the time. The Paterson Savings Institute was the first savings bank in the east to have a policy of distributing profits to stockholders rather than to depositors. New Jersey Bank was the first bank in the state to have an international department and the first to offer automated teller machines.

Paterson and Passaic County are not merely the settings for a series of industrial firsts but rather the launching site of a new, industrial society—the place where many of the characteristics, both social and economic, of a changing society were shaped.

Tim's Fireworks Store was decked out for the centennial celebration of 1892 in Paterson. Courtesy, Passaic County Historical Society

Chapter VI

A County Shaped Like An Hourglass

Facing page: A Sunday outing for the well-to-do of Paterson in the 1870s included a promenade on the chasm bridge. Courtesy, The Paterson Museum

In the years before the Civil War, the United States Congress fought many bitter battles over admission of new states to the Union. The Northerners wanted no new slave states and the Southerners wanted no free states, since new neither side wanted the other to gain two more seats in the Senate. The only compromise was to admit two states at a time—one slave, one free—thus preserving the balance of power.

New Jersey was similarly divided into northern and southern factions, although slavery was not the issue. Instead, there were thirteen counties when New Jersey became a state: six were urban and situated in the north, and seven were predominantly rural and southern. The rural and southern counties, having different needs and interests than those of the more industrialized and populous north, closely guarded their voting advantage in the state senate, which then consisted of one member for each county. Thus it is not surprising that more than forty years passed before the legislature exercised its power to create a new county. Warren County, approved in 1824, was more north than south geographically, but it was largely agricultural and therefore somewhat in tune with the interests of the southern counties.

In the early 1830s residents of West Milford Township became discontented being governed by Bergen County, especially since the county seat in Hackensack was difficult to reach by the transportation facilities of those days. West Milford joined with the township of Pompton in petitioning the legislature to be separated from Bergen County and to be created as a new county of Pompton. At the same time, the townships of Paterson, Manchester, and Ackquackanonk objected to being governed from Newark as part of Essex County. They petitioned to be set apart as Passaic County. However, legislators from the southern part of the state had no interest in creating two more northern counties and the petitions languished for several years.

The legislature eventually worked out a compromise. The two petitions of the five townships in the north would be consolidated into one, and a new southern county, Atlantic, would also be created. By an act adopted February 7, 1837, the counties of Atlantic and Passaic were established.

This compromise proved viable if not perfect for all concerned. Bergen and Essex counties, from which the five townships that became Passaic County were separated, raised no objections at the time. Fifty to seventy-five years later Essex might have

Right: The Passaic County jail is shown here in about 1890. Courtesy, Passaic County Historical Society

Below: With a fallen tree as a perhaps symbolic prop, the tax assessors of Passaic County posed about 1890. Pictured are Thomas E. Smith, James Johnson, W.D. Plunck, Thomas H. Risk, and John Colfer. Courtesy, Passaic County Historical Society

had second thoughts when Passaic County and Essex spent years in litigation over water rights and sewers.

The merging of the two petitions was not really a happy marriage for the five townships. The two upper townships were in many ways unlike the lower townships with which they were united. Even today the upper and lower townships have different outlooks, different geography, and different political and social orientation. The upper townships then were sparsely settled and agricultural, and their priorities in terms of government had little in common with those of the fast-growing commercial, industrial, and urban lower townships, which demanded more money and services.

Geographically, the merger of the five townships created a county shaped like an hourglass. From north to south it is only twenty-seven miles long, and its narrowest width, at Pompton Lakes, is less than three miles. It is the state's fourth-smallest county in area but does have the distinction of being one of only three counties out of twenty-one to share a land boundary with another state. The State of New Jersey, bordered on the west by the Delaware River, on the south by Delaware Bay, and on the east by the Atlantic Ocean and the Hudson River, has its only land boundary to the north, dividing it from New York State, and that line is but forty-eight miles long. Sussex, Passaic, and Bergen counties share that line.

Paterson was selected as the county seat, for it was the largest community. Thomas Gordon in his *Gazetteer of the State of New Jersey* in 1834 termed Paterson a "thriving manufacturing town" with 765 dwellings, seventy-six stores, and 9,085 residents. There were two weekly newspapers and nine churches. Twenty cotton mills employed 1,646 people, the Morris Canal was in operation, and Paterson could boast of being the terminus of a railroad, the Paterson and Hudson River, only the second one chartered in the state. It was a bit of unfortunate timing that in the county's first year of existence the Panic of 1837 seized the nation's economy and almost wiped out

The blizzard of 1888 buried John Denby's grocery store, as well as the rest of the county and the East Coast. Courtesy, The Paterson Museum

Paterson before it could start functioning as the seat of county government.

Two of the original five townships, Ackquackanonk and Manchester, have since disappeared from the map, and of the remaining three only West Milford formerly a part of Pompton until 1834, is still a township. West Milford had been an independent township for three years when the county was created. Pompton was established as a township in 1797 and is now a borough. Paterson, originally a township carved out of Ackquackanonk, became a city in 1851.

The vanished townships of Ackquackanonk and Manchester actually and ironically *grew* out of existence. Passaic broke away from Ackquackanonk in 1866 and became a city in 1873. Little Falls, still a township, separated from Ackquackanonk in 1868. Consequently, only a scattering of villages and sections remained of Ackquackanonk: Delawanna, Athenia, Allwood, Cloverdale, Richfield, Albion Place, and Clifton. In 1917 all these combined to form the city of Clifton, and Ackquackanonk was no more.

Manchester disappeared in 1908 when its last territory incorporated as the Borough of Haledon. Previously it had lost Wayne Township in 1847, Totowa Borough and Hawthorne Borough in 1898, and North Haledon and Prospect Park boroughs in 1901. Manchester survives now only as a street name, and as the name of a regional high school.

The year 1918 saw the boroughs of Bloomingdale, Wanaque, and Ringwood become independent of Pompton Township. In 1914 West Paterson Borough split from Little Falls Township. By 1986 Passaic County had sixteen municipalities: three cities (Paterson, Passaic, and Clifton), three townships (Little Falls, West Milford, and Wayne), and ten boroughs.

The forms of local government in New Jersey are not consistently determined by the type of municipality—cities, townships, boroughs, and villages—as there are variations in each category, and variations within variations.

Little Falls has one of the few remaining old-fashioned township forms of government. There is a five-member Township Committee, the members of which are elected at large and called committeemen. In every other Passaic County municipality members of the governing body are called councilmen, except in Hawthorne, which operates under the commission form of government and has commissioners. In Little Falls and in Hawthorne the committeemen or commissioners elect one of their own number as mayor. All other municipalities in the county have direct election of their mayors, except Clifton and West Milford, where the council elects one of its members as mayor.

Until a charter revision roughly twenty years ago, Paterson had a unique form of government under a special charter granted by the legislature. Paterson had a Board of Aldermen whose powers were limited to such matters as granting licenses and appointing constables. The real power of government lay with boards appointed by the mayor, such as the a Board of Finance, Board of Public Works, and Board of Police and Fire. The law has provided that in case of the death or resignation of the mayor, the president of the Board of Finance will succeed as mayor—an event that happened twice in the 1950s and 1960s.

County government in New Jersey has several forms, but all include a legislative body called the Board of Chosen Freeholders, a term coming down from English common law. Originally such a board consisted only of landowners (freeholders). Since colonial times the boards of freeholders have exercised both legislative and executive functions, and in Passaic County they still do. Some counties have adopted a form of government that provides for an elected county executive. While some counties elect by districts, Passaic County

The Wayne, New Jersey, post office is seen on a postcard about 1900. Courtesy, Passaic County Historical Society

The Little Falls Municipal Building is seen in the 1930s. Courtesy, Passaic County Historical Society

elects its seven freeholders at large and there are still overtones of competition between the upper and lower municipalities in the voting. On both the 1985 and 1986 boards, there were six members from the lower section and only one from the northern section, thus keeping alive an old rivalry.

With its small geographic size and its distinctive shape, Passaic County has been subject to gerrymandering throughout the years in laying out both legislative and congressional districts. Of its five state assembly districts, none is wholly within the county, although two are predominantly Passaic County-oriented. All involve towns in Essex, Bergen, or Morris counties. It has three congressional districts. One congressman is currently a resident of the county, although his district also covers some municipalities in Bergen and Essex counties. Part of the county, however, is represented by a congressman who lives in Morris, and another portion is represented by a congressman from Bergen.

By virtue of its creation, there is no single Passaic County—there are really two. This dual personality carries over into every facet of life and politics. Suburban development has spread to the upper county, but the land is still noted for its scenic beauty, its water supply potential, and its many excellent recreational attractions. The townships are working to keep it that way. The northern area is rugged country, with the third-highest point of elevation in the state (1,490 feet in the Bearfort Mountains in West Milford). Thousands of acres of undeveloped land are legally locked into the watersheds, to provide water for the City of Newark and the North Jersey District Water Commission. South of Pompton Lakes, where the land flattens out toward sea level, industry, commerce, and population have concentrated into eleven municipalities.

Passaic is the only New Jersey county with a name of Indian derivation, and it is one of only two named for a river (the other being Hudson County. How the name Passaic came to be adopted by the city of Passaic has been related by William W. Scott in *Passaic and Its Environs.* It was originally called Ackquankanonk Landing or Ackquackanonk Bridge. The name was used by General George Washington in his correspondence from there in November 1776. In 1814 the first post office for the township of Ackquackanonk was established at Ackquackanonk Landing.

Ackquackanonk Landing was known for a time as Paterson Landing and, infrequently, as Quacknick, a distorted form of Ackquackanonk. When the Erie Railroad came to Ackquackanonk Landing in the late 1830s, its station agent was named Huyler, and Erie timetables referred to the place as Huyler's Station, and so read the name on the station itself.

This confusion in names irritated several

of the leading citizens of the community, among them one Alfred Speer, an inventor known for a moving sidewalk he designed for Broadway in New York City, but from which he was unable to capitalize, and the owner of large vineyards, a winery, and a hotel near the landing. On February 15, 1854, Speer called a meeting of like-minded citizens and proposed that the place be named Passaic, securing at the meeting a large number of signatures on a petition to the postmaster general. Sentiment for the change was not universal in the community, as many traditionalists favored retention of Ackquackanonk or Ackquackanonk Landing. There were others who preferred a name different from that of the county or the river. The Erie was not anxious to reprint its timetables to change the name of one station stop.

But Speer carried the petition to Washington, D.C., where on April 25, 1854, the postmaster general approved an order making the name Passaic official. Speer had two large signs painted, and by night he hung one on the Erie station, the other on the post office. Despite objections, the signs stayed up, and the name stuck.

Finally, there is the Wayne Township section known as Preakness, through which flows the Preakness Brook, which was named after a racehorse. Born and raised in the area, the fame of the racehorse Preakness was so great that a top Thoroughbred stakes race—the Preakness Stakes, second jewel of racing's Triple Crown—was named in his honor.

Rent asunder as it may be topographically, politically, and economically, Passaic is a county that has many attractions and a rich history. Even its shape makes it unique.

Houses of worship in Passaic County have ranged from the ornate to the ramshackle. This is the Wells Street Baptist Church in the 1880s, which was photographed by Reid Studio. For obvious reasons, the church was known as the "wigwam." Courtesy, The Paterson Museum

Above: Although Upper Passaic County in the 1880s was increasingly industrial, life in the lower part of Passaic County remained rural, quiet, but nevertheless hardworking. Courtesy, Passaic County Historical Society

Right: Until the last two or three decades, upper Passaic County was rustic. This engraving appears to be near Wayne or Pequannock. Courtesy, Vincent Marchese

Chapter VII

Wm MILLS Jr FURNITURE VAN
ANK St. PATERSON. N. J.

From Stagecoaches to Interstates

The history of transportation in Passaic County begins with the rivers. The rivers fueled the mills, factories, and the Society of Useful Manufactures in the county. The first settlements evolved around the waterways. Roads were poor and in earlier days never amounted to more than two parallel ruts overlaid on a deer or Indian trail.

Originally, roads were simply created by frequent use of paths created by the Leni-Lenapes, such as the Minisink Trail that ran through Wayne. Progress on the Colony's first roads was slow and often painful. When not on foot, the settlers used oxcarts, horses, or wagons to travel between churches, mills, and other settlements. If the roads were dry, passengers were thrown against hard board seats each time their wagon wheels hit a rock or rut; in wet weather they often had to climb down from the wagon to lighten the load and to help pull the horses and wagon out of the mud. Therefore, traffic on the river, from the beginning, remained heavy well into the twentieth century. Acquackanonk Landing provided wharfs and docks for private vessels, as well as for cargo boats carrying lumber, produce, and other goods to and from Newark and New York City. Iron from the mines at Ringwood and Pompton was transported to Acquackanonk Landing and then shipped by boat. The end of the nineteenth century saw a new addition to the river vehicles. John Stevens and Nicholas Roosevelt built the *Polacca*, the first steamboat not only on the Passaic, but in America, which made its trial run in 1798. This early experiment led the way for Robert Fulton's steamboat in 1807.

Later, in the nineteenth century, pleasure and excursion boats added to river traffic. Boat races and regattas were popular, as well as many rowing clubs. Local residents also bought tickets for excursions on boats like the *Passaic Queen*, which ran regularly during the day between Passaic and Newark, but at night and on weekends carried revellers and picnickers on festive trips. Excursion boats also took passengers between Newark and Acquackanonk to see the sights along the river's banks. During this period the Passaic River was also used for recreation, with its shores boasting palatial homes and immaculately kept grounds, drawing thousands of sightseers. Additionally, fishermen and shellfish gatherers used the river extensively. Until it was fished out and killed by pollution, the Passaic River was popular for all sorts of mussels. Hunting freshwater pearls, some very large, drew thousands to Passaic

Facing page: In the 1890s, this incredibly ornate wagon delivered furniture. The painting on the side is simply inscribed Passaic Falls, Paterson, N.J. *Courtesy, Passaic County Historical Society*

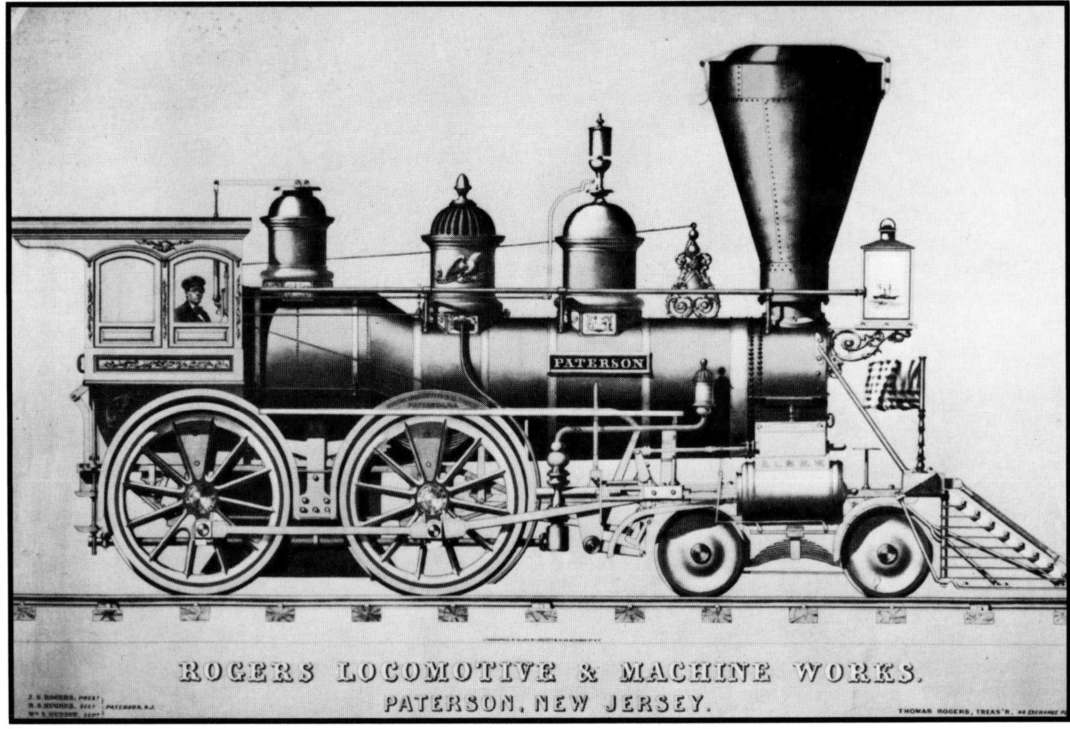

State-of-the-art transportation in the 1860s, a Rogers 4-4-0 locomotive bore a steamship painted on its headlamp. Some locomotives were even more elaborately decorated. Courtesy, Passaic County Historical Society

County to wade in its rivers in a sort of gold rush.

Unfortunately, the dawn of the railroad age meant that the economic value of the rivers in the county lay solely in their use as an open cesspit for the factories and mines. Chemicals and filth were poured into the Passaic River in such amounts that south of Passaic the river was pure sludge. A Franklin Institute (Philadelphia) study in the 1880s found that the fumes from the river were felling people with all kinds of ailments. The study, an early ecological examination, recommended a host of measures for the crippled waterway. But it was years before any serious cleanup attempts were made. By 1840 the rivers had taken a backseat to trains and improved roads.

Original road traffic was crude by comparison to movement by river. It was difficult to wring money out of the townships or the state to maintain roads and bridges. Money was scarce in colonial New Jersey. Bond issues were unattractive to voters. Usually, a lottery was held to pay for road work. Later towns or counties had responsibility for and jurisdiction over roads that ran through their land. In the beginning of the nineteenth century, the New Jersey state legislature began to grant charters to private companies to establish and run turnpikes. These companies had power to take over existing roads or build new roads and in either case could charge tolls for their use.

The way these toll collecting points were set up led to the term "turnpike." A pole, or pike, was placed across the road so that vehicles would stop to pay the toll. Once payment was received the pike would be moved or turned away so that the vehicle could pass—an early forerunner of the automated gates on modern toll booths. These first turnpike companies had to charge high rates in order to make a profit and to compensate for the large number of travelers—including those going to church, or the mills—who were exempt from the toll. Generally, a rider on horseback paid one halfpenny per mile. Coaches were charged per horse at the rate of one cent per mile per horse up to four horses; vehicles having larger teams were charged at an even higher rate.

The first road in Passaic ran to Newark

Temporary walkways accommodated "sidewalk directors" during the building of the West Street Bridge at the Broomhead Mill in Paterson in November of 1897. Courtesy, Passaic County Historical Society

The Pompton Turnpike in Wayne, New Jersey, is pictured in about 1910. Courtesy, Passaic County Historical Society

The post office and general store of Mountain View, New Jersey, was photographed between 1900 and 1910. A horse-drawn mail wagon is visible at left. Courtesy, Passaic County Historical Society

and was in use by 1707. The second, a church road, was laid out in 1714. Ten years later the third road, Van Houten Avenue, was created. Other Passaic County roads have existed since before the Revolutionary War. These include the Newark-Pompton Turnpike and Ratzer and Valley roads in Wayne. In North Haledon, High Mountain Road was in use in the early 1700s. As late as 1898, the only paved roads in Hawthorne were Godwinville Road (now Goffle), Lafayette Avenue, and Goetchius Lane (now Lincoln Ave). As Passaic County is crisscrossed with rivers, roads could not run very far without encountering a body of water. The earliest method of river crossing was by ferry. Often, the ferryman would keep a tavern for the comfort of travelers waiting for transport. Tired, hungry, and thirsty, weary travelers would spend freely in the taverns. A law was passed in 1779 to prevent the ferrymen/tavern keepers from deliberately operating infrequently to keep customers in the taverns for as long as possible.

If a river had to be crossed at a point where no ferry was available, travelers made use of whatever was nearby. Often they were able to locate only a canoe or an unstable boat just large enough to carry the passengers while their livestock swam alongside. This led to the legend of long tails on horses. If a boat tipped while crossing, the legend said, the capsized traveler could grab onto his horse's tail and hitch a ride to shore. The longer the tail, the less chance of being kicked in the process.

Even superstition created another obstacle to travel on the Hamburg Turnpike. Legend had it that a "Witch of Preakness" stood in her doorway preventing anyone from driving cattle past her home unless they first greeted her, or, according to a variation of the story, created a sign with sticks in the road.

As overland travel became more extensive, regular stagecoach routes were established. Just before the start of the Revolution, most open wagons were replaced by the enclosed Conestoga wagons usually associated with the West. As early as 1774, several stage lines served Paterson and Acquackanonk, running frequently to Newark and Paulus Hook (now Jersey City) and Abraham Godwin ran a stage from his tavern in Paterson (then Acquackanonk) to Jersey City twice a week, a distance of nineteen miles. Godwin charged two shillings and ninepence for a one-way ride between these points and his stage did a good business transporting sightseers to the Great Falls. The falls continued to be a major tourist attraction, sometimes compared to Africa's Victoria Falls. The Archdeacon family also capitalized on this natural attraction, establishing nearby a restaurant and hotel called the "Cottage on the Cliff." Other competitors were Peter Sloat, Samuel Pope, and Noah Sexton, who all ran coaches to the Hoboken Ferry. Later, John Fione began another line on the run to Newark. New service also opened up between Belleville and Passaic.

The stagecoach drivers themselves were very colorful. They were constant—if not always accurate—bearers of the latest news and brought mail with them. Younger residents looked up to the drivers as romantic figures, or even heroes. Walter Van Hoesin, in *Early Taverns and Stagecoach Days in New Jersey,* writes of one driver whose method of steering involved spitting tobacco at the ear of the lead horse.

Increase in travel, particularly beyond the one-day trip range, gave rise to a number of taverns. Some of the first taverns served as "warming houses," providing respite between unheated morning and afternoon Sunday church services. Such respite was available only to men, however, as women remained behind in church. Gradually, tavern keepers also began to provide accommodations for travelers who had earlier been put up in private homes, a service important enough for the state legislature to require each community on a stage route to

John Cronin's tavern near Main Street was photographed before the turn of the century. Courtesy, Passaic County Historical Societ

The men and women of a coachmaker's concern posed in the 1870s for this photo, which was probably taken in Paterson. Families lived in the building as well. Courtesy, Passaic County Historical Society

provide a tavern for travelers.

When railroads replaced stagecoaches, many taverns went out of business. Two of the best-known taverns in Passaic were the Tap House on the Hill, which had originally served the warming function for the Dutch Reformed Church, and the White Horse Tavern, or Eutaw House, later called the Century House. Cornelius Vreeland also established a tavern to serve travelers in Great Notch in 1798. The tavern served a civic purpose as well. It provided a site for court sessions, town meetings, and elections. Simeon Brown bought the tavern in 1818 and sold it to Henry Piaget in 1839.

When the Erie Railroad began running in 1832, one of its depots was on Main Avenue between Passaic Street and Park Place. The owner of a saloon and lunchroom there found that rail passengers were less interested in stopping for food and drink than stage passengers had been. So, as his business worsened, he adapted to the times and became a ticket agent.

By the mid-1700s ferries could no longer accommodate the volume of traffic seeking to cross the county's rivers, and local governments began to consider the possibility of constructing bridges. The Revolutionary War bridge in Acquackanonk, used by American troops when retreating from the British, was constructed sometime before 1741. First capable of supporting only foot traffic, this bridge was rebuilt several times in the ensuing years in order to strengthen it or to repair damage caused by ice and floods.

In the 1790s the New Jersey legislature granted charters to companies to build additional bridges over the Passaic and Hackensack rivers. These companies were also granted the right to collect tolls. A person crossing on foot paid four cents, with prices rising to thirty-nine cents for a coach and four horses—a charge widely considered excessive.

When railroad bridges were built to carry the then-unheard-of weights of lo-

The Franklin House Hotel, photographed in the 1860s, was an important lodging and gathering place. Located near West and Main, it was a descendant of the Keller Tavern of the 1820s. Courtesy, Passaic County Historical Society

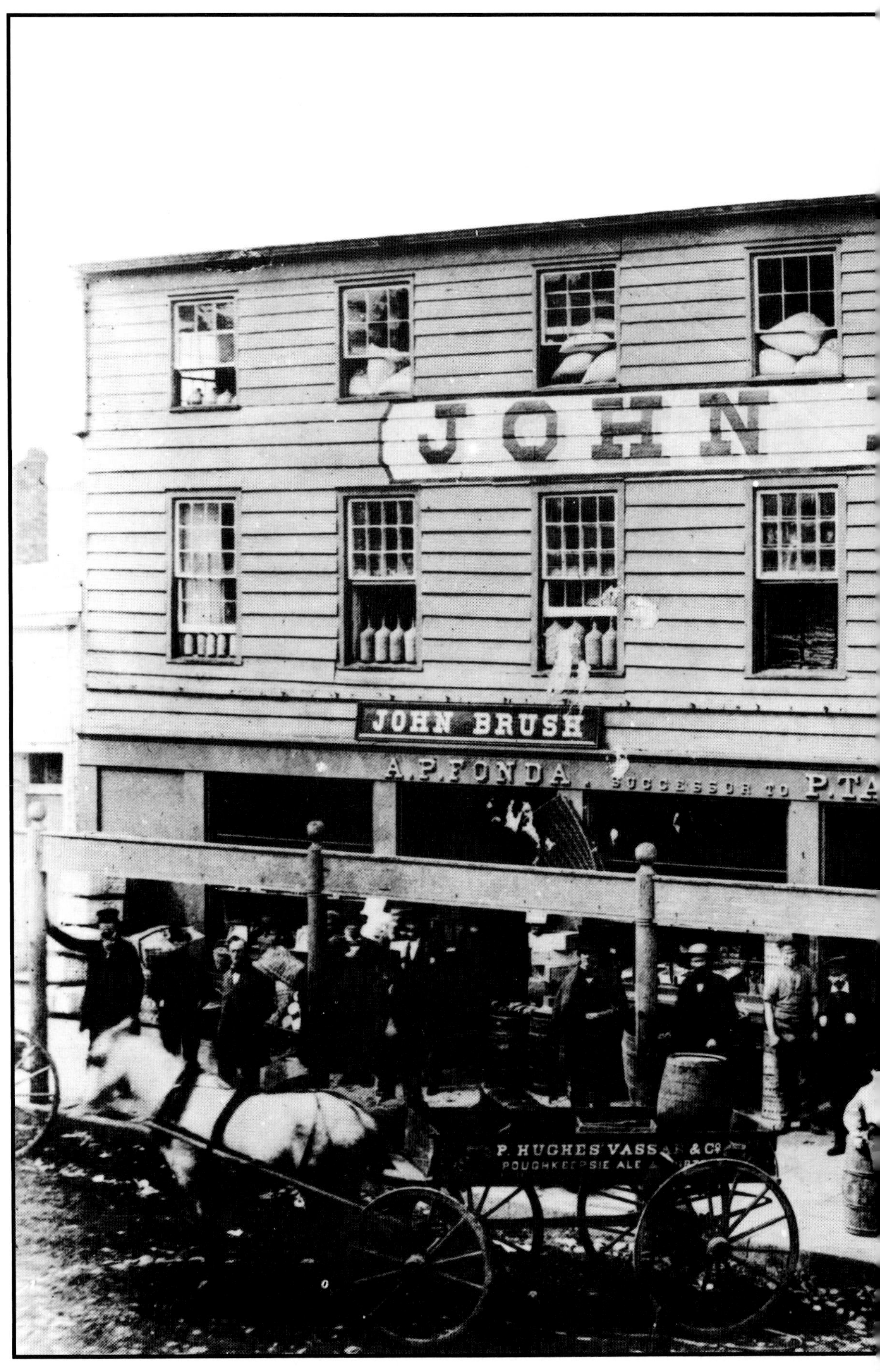
JOHN
JOHN BRUSH
A.P.FONDA
SUCCESSOR TO
P. HUGHES

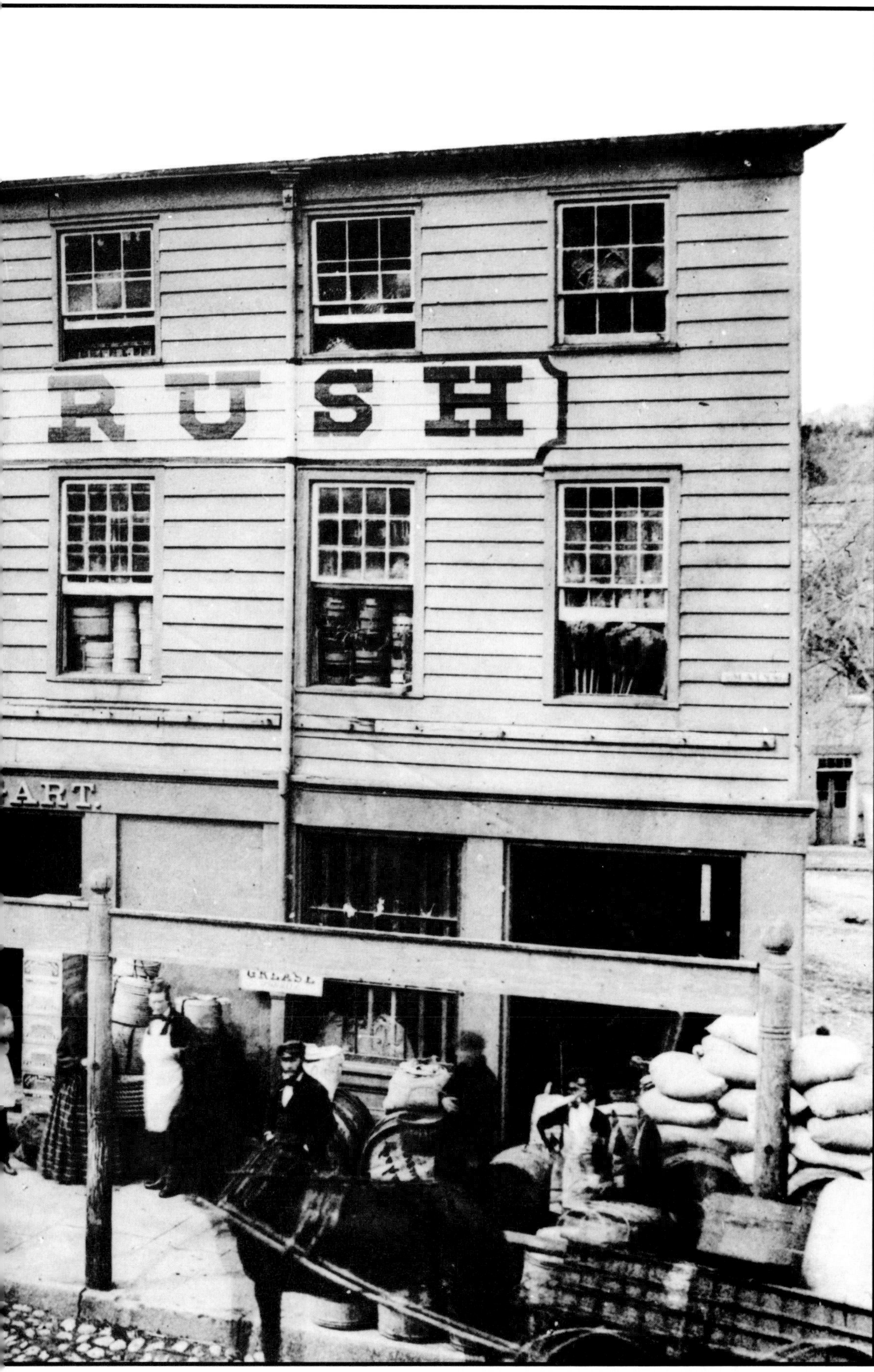

When John Brush had the Reid Studio photograph his store around 1860, he carefully arranged his products in the windows and on the sidewalk. He seems to have sold just about everything from brooms to bottles to grease. Courtesy, The Paterson Museum

As the United States expanded across the continent, weather in the East brought about the development of new technology, such as this giant rotary snow plow produced by the Leslie Works in Paterson. Courtesy, The Paterson Museum

comotives and rolling stock, public authorities insisted on proof of structural safety. The Paterson and Hudson Railroad tested the Weasel Bridge in Passaic with two locomotives, two hopper cars loaded with gravel, and several laborers all placed on the bridge simultaneously. That the bridge held the weight instilled confidence and brought public acceptance.

Despite the introduction of bridges, turnpikes, and railroads, the basic road system was still in poor shape. Particularly after the heavy traffic of the War of 1812, public discontent over the condition of the roads in the area reached new heights. Faced with the prospect of continually deteriorating roadways, George P. McCulloch of Morristown conceived the idea of building a canal to link the Passaic and Delaware rivers and thereby support both passenger travel and cargo shipping. A group of private investors soon formed the Morris Canal and Banking Company and, in 1824, received a charter from the state legislature to build the canal. Once the charter was granted, the first of the 1,100 men who constructed the canal, most of whom were Irish immigrants, went to work: twelve hours a day, six days a week, almost entirely with picks and shovels. Earning one dollar a day, their wages were paid partly in cash and partly in whiskey, as was the custom. To meet the payroll, the investors issued their own money, as no national currency yet existed.

Canal construction ran over budget. Although first estimated at slightly more than $800,000, the final construction cost was more than two million dollars. The first trip made on the canal was in 1831, and 1832 saw the first full season of use. Traveling the full length of the ninety-mile

An early steam shovel digs gravel for the rail-beds of the New Jersey Midland Railroad at Sandy Hill near Paterson around 1875. Courtesy, Passaic County Historical Society

canal would take travelers through the Passaic County towns of Pompton Plains, Little Falls, West Paterson, Paterson, and Clifton. Boats were pulled by horses or mules who walked on a towpath beside the water and were harnessed to the boat by a towline. It took five days to complete the trip from Phillipsburg to Newark Bay.

The Morris Canal crossed a number of rivers lying in its path and these junctures provided an interesting feature of canal navigation. At Little Falls, the canal crossed the Passaic river about 200 feet from the Beattie rug mill. A stone aqueduct took the canal across the river and from this point it ran behind the Main Street stores in Little Falls, crossed Paterson Avenue, ran over Maple and East Main streets to near Francisco Avenue, then over the Peckman River, backtracked under the bridge at Lower Long Hill Road, ran along Browertown Road to West Paterson, and finally Garrett Mountain. The canal also crossed the Pompton River, this time passing through a wooden aqueduct that was 236 feet long.

As the canal's height changed a total of 2,134 feet throughout its length, McCulloch needed to design a system that would allow efficient movement of boats up and down inclines. Sometimes changes in elevation were accomplished by using a series of locks running alongside the main canal. On particularly steep inclines, boats were actually pulled from the water and carried uphill on a cradle running along railroad-like tracks and powered by a water-driven turbine. At the top of the hill, the boat was pushed back into the water to continue on its way. This transfer gave the mules a break for feeding as they were unhitched and walked to meet the boat again. Horses sometimes pulled the boats, but mules tended to hold up to the hard

Pleasure boating, as shown here near the West Street Bridge in the 1880s, brought money and tourists to Passaic County in the 1800s. People did so at their own peril, as the fumes from the polluted Passaic River could peel paint from houses two blocks away. Courtesy, Passaic County Historical Society

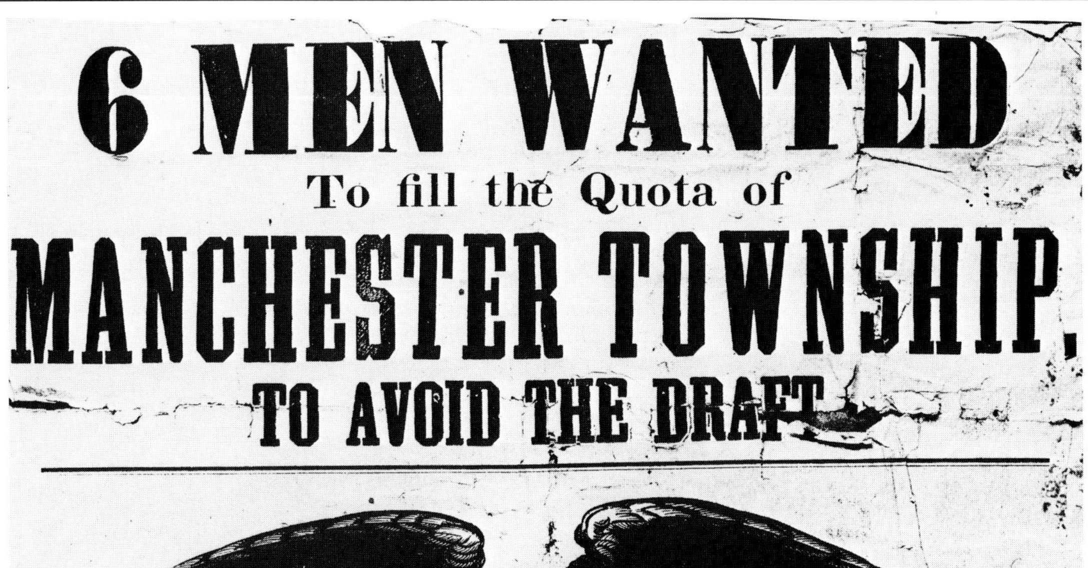

Late in the Civil War, casualties were high and New Jersey's troops were hit hard. When the draft came, it was unpopular. Townships hired men to fill their draft quotas, rather than have "men of quality" hauled off at random. Courtesy, Passaic County Historical Society

In addition to sending young men to fight the Confederates, Passaic County sent locomotives and other war matériel. Without the power of the railroads, the Union might have lost the Civil War. This photo of a Rogers locomotive was taken at City Point, near Washington, D.C., on September 1, 1864. Courtesy, The Paterson Museum

work better.

A boat traveling the whole length of the canal went through twenty-eight locks and twenty-three inclined planes. The locks and incline passages were no doubt among the features leading English diarist Frances Trollope to describe the canal as "a very interesting work, it is one among a thousand which prove the people of America to be the most enterprising in the world."

Most of the boats on the canal carried freight, most often coal, and frequently iron ore from the mines. These cargo boats were 87.5 feet long and 10.5 feet wide. The boats were too wide to be turned in the canal; if a change of direction had to be made, it was done in specially widened areas called "turning basins." Unfortunately, these turning basins were also allowed to become graveyards for boats no longer needed.

While conceived as an industrial cargo route, the Morris Canal was equally popular for the recreation it supported. Canalling was enjoyed by entire families, with steering the father's responsibility and one of the children leading the family mule. Those who didn't own a boat could pay a fare and ride between Newark and Paterson. Canoers used the canal, too, their occupants choosing between using the locks to overcome the changes in height or carrying the canoe to the next level section. Some people purchased season passes to the canal and locks and some paid on a per trip basis. Swimming was another pleasure—as was ice skating in the winter.

No one used the canal on Sundays, however, as it was closed to give the lock keepers a day off. This also allowed missionaries to preach to canal work crews who sometimes lived on maintenance boats for weeks at a time while digging out silt and weeds accumulated on the canal floor.

Despite its engineering marvels, the canal was really only profitable during the Civil War. Railroad rolling stock was needed near the battlefront and rail operators planned with canal owners to have canals carry cargo. But this arrangement did not last past the end of the Civil War. Profiting

Lieutenant Hugh Irish fought in the Civil War and never returned. His name was adopted by a local veterans' organization. Courtesy, The Paterson Museum

most from the canal were the owners of real estate or businesses beside it. Suddenly served by an easy, economical shipping route, the value of these properties increased greatly, and canal-generated water power also benefited adjoining industries. But when railroads began to compete for profits shortly after its completion, the canal's days were already numbered. Railroads were faster, cheaper, and had an added advantage—they operated throughout the year, while ice closed the canal in the winter.

Economic losses took their toll, and the Morris Canal and Banking Company was forced to lease the canal to the Lehigh Valley Railroad in 1871. The railroad could not make a profit either, so the canal and its associated rights were sold to the state of New Jersey. The state legislature resolved to abandon the canal in 1903, but no action was taken. In 1924 the Morris Canal and Banking Company was appointed trustee and directed to bring canal operations to an end. The Morris Canal and Banking Company was not formally dissolved until 1973, when canal property reverted to the state.

While the canal was never a financial success, its contribution to the region's history cannot be overlooked. People owning land near the canal had access to markets; more people were encouraged to move in to sparsely populated areas; and land values went up. Water from the canal encouraged mills to operate nearby, which increased employment and farm production. To acknowledge the Morris Canal's role in Passaic County history, West Paterson volunteers restored a canal section for the Bicentennial Celebration of 1976.

The real culprit in the demise of the canals was the steam locomotive. The Paterson and Hudson Railroad experienced a very modest beginning in 1831. Originally, it merely ferried passengers between stage stops in Paterson and Passaic for connections with the Newark stagecoaches.

Around 1889 the owner and employees of a Paterson newspaper and job printer posed outside their building. As was usual for the time, they are arranged by rank and job classification. Courtesy, Passaic County Historical Society

During the Spanish-American War of 1898, E.T. Bell, Jr., (center) served in the 2nd Regiment of the New Jersey Volunteer Infantry. This photo probably was taken in training because the caps of his subordinates were not worn either in Florida or at the front. Courtesy, Passaic County Historical Society

What apparently was the first railroad drawbridge was built on this route. Philemon Dickerson was the company's first president and the initial stock offering was fifty dollars per share. It sold out in no time.

The Paterson-Ramapo Railroad ran through the county from Jersey City to within a mile of the New York State border. The route was plotted by William Gibbs McNeill and George Washington Whistler, the father of artist James Abbott McNeill Whistler. Whistler married McNeill's sister. McNeill had surveyed and supervised the construction of six previous railroads, among them the Boston and Providence, the Boston and Lowell, and the Boston and Susquehanna lines.

The first railroad cars appeared in Passaic in the spring of 1832, which caused great excitement and drew spectators. The two pieces of rolling stock were displayed in a car barn at Main and Prospect streets. Thirty feet long and painted bright red, each car could seat forty people. Pulled by eight horses, the cars made their first trip in June. To allay public concern about this new form of travel, the company assured the riding public that the horses were "gentle" and the drivers "careful." The only surviving car of this type today is still running at the Strasburg Railroad Museum in Strasburg, Pennsylvania.

After a brief horse-drawn period, the first steam locomotive arrived, in pieces, from England. It was named the *McNeill* after the railroad's chief architect. This was the same engine that Thomas Rogers put together in 1835, and from which he learned the basics that would make Paterson a leading locomotive producer. For two more years, passengers could choose between horses and locomotive as the preferred means of propulsion. Timetables listed the power source for travelers' convenience.

As with any new technology, early train travel was not easy or accident-free. Cars frequently derailed and passengers were expected to help right them on the tracks. But railroads played a key role in the growth of local industry in Passaic County. They made it possible for workers to live further from work, which expanded the suburbs, and they opened the northern section of the county to recreational use on a large scale. The Montclair and Greenwood Lake Railway, which ran through Pompton, was in large part responsible for the emergence of Pompton Lakes and other upcounty communities. In industrial terms, the railroad lines made possible huge factories, where rails linked different shops and hauled fabric rolls, iron ingots, and various other bulk cargoes with ease. Without

This machine, used for melting snow, was self-propelled. It was manufactured by the Snow and Ice Liquefying Company of Paterson in about 1910. Todd Rafferty is shown holding the whippletree. Courtesy, Passaic County Historical Society

them, much of Passaic County's industrial development would have come to nothing. Finally, Rogers' locomotives, as well as Cooke and Danforth's and Grant's made Passaic County a nationwide powerhouse.

Like the canals, though, the railroads, too, were doomed. Owners of the lines engaged in such criminal chicanery with stock issues, freight rebates, and price wars that by 1900, the public was fed up with the sometimes illegal and unethical practices of Cornelius Vanderbilt, Jay Gould, Jim Hill, and Jim Fiske, among others. The Interstate Commerce Commission regulated the railroads, beginning in 1887. When trucks and planes appeared, Congress voted subsidies and tax exemptions for them, but not for the rail lines. Bogged down in taxes and facing unequal competition, the railroads entered their long downhill slide culminated by the depression. The Erie Railroad, which never in its history showed a profit on paper, had run trains through Passaic County for decades. Eventually, it was forced to merge with the Delaware, Lackawanna, and Western Railroad to form the Erie-Lackawanna. CONRAIL took over the Erie-Lackawanna lines in 1976, and in 1978, New Jersey took ownership from CONRAIL. The last rail line in downtown Passaic closed in 1963.

A related transport industry was the trolley line. New Jersey's first electric trolley car began in Passaic in 1890. The car was owned and operated by the Passaic, Garfield, and Clifton Railway Company, and it connected those three towns. The complete trip, one-way, took twenty minutes. Trolleys later linked residents of Totowa, Prospect Park, Haledon, North Haledon, and West Paterson with shopping and jobs in downtown Passaic and Paterson. By 1908 Paterson had thirteen trolley lines with 100 cars, making 1,288 trips a day on thirty-seven miles of track. Hawthorne, too, had its streetcars, running between 1910 and 1928 along Wagaraw Road. As a popular conveyance for passengers, the

These teachers taught at School No. 12 in Paterson. Seen at the top is Rachel Van Blarcom. Left to right, top to bottom are: Carrie MacNab; Annie Broome; Charlotte Cuddeback; Margaret Suttle; Elizabeth J. Sautter; Edith M. Tuttle; Mary Halliday; Ettie Smith; Elizabeth Reilly; Margaret Gowdy; Jessie MacFarlan; Louise Olmstead; Annie E. Taylor; and Principal Albert Chadwick. Courtesy, Passaic County Historical Society

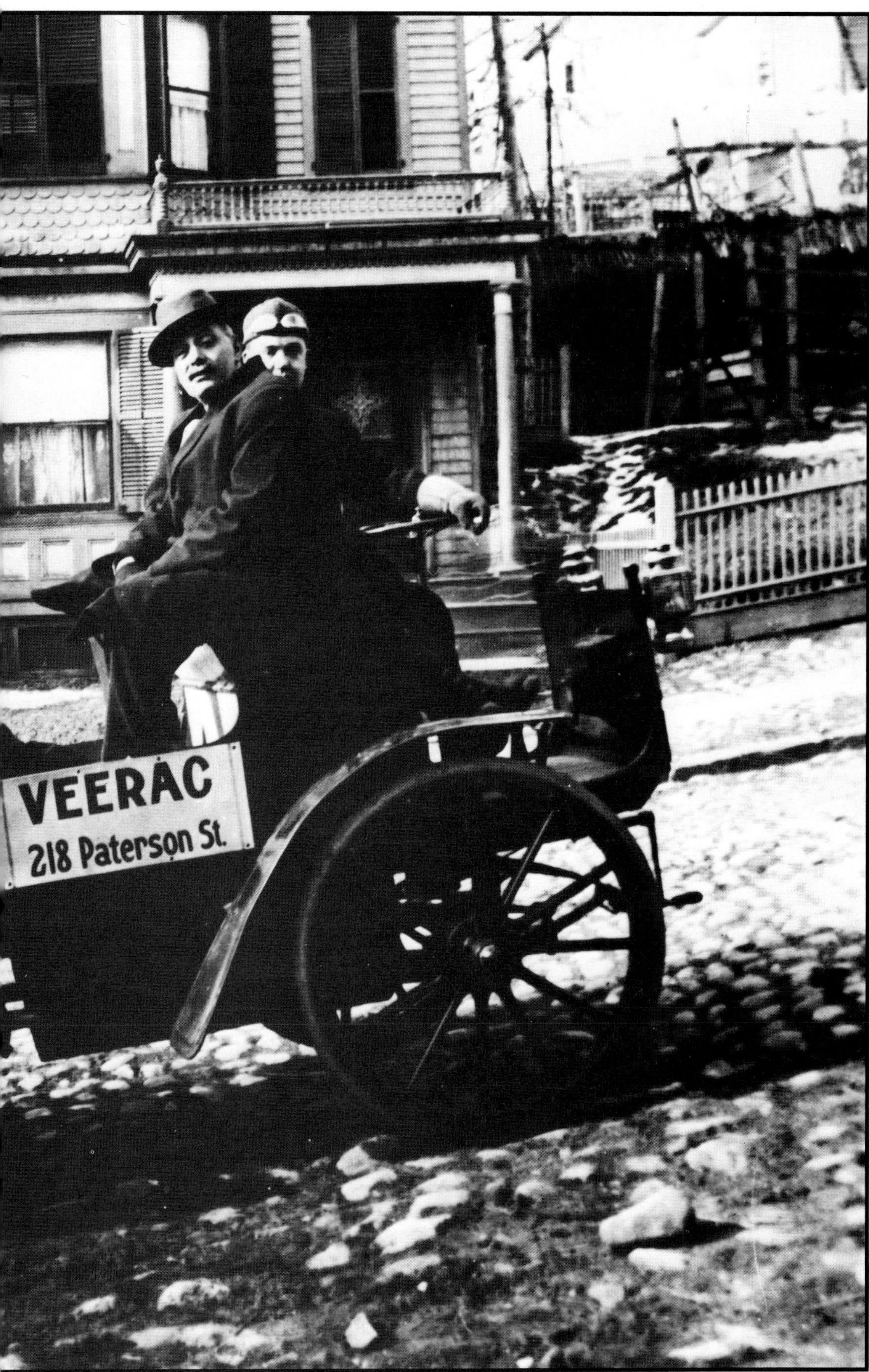

The internal combustion engine was popular in Paterson. This 1910-1915 truck made transport cheaper, faster, and more reliable, but thin tires on cobblestones must have been a bone-bruising experience. Courtesy, Passaic County Historical Society

trolleys succumbed in turn to the automobile, which was inexpensive, went anywhere without tracks, and appealed to the American's traditional sense of individuality.

Automobiles were a mixed blessing, allowing many people to work in the more urban cities like Paterson and Passaic, while living in quickly developing suburbs. Travel between Paterson and Wayne had historically been difficult, for example, since trolleys were unable to cross a ridge in the Watchung Mountains. Automobiles were readily able to negotiate the ridge and greatly improved access between the two cities. Improved transportation brought enough people to the northern part of Passaic County to support nine hotels between Pompton and Newfoundland. As happened in so many other places, the advent of the automobile allowed greater mobility, traffic patterns began to change, and merchants in the cities lost much of their retail business to suburban shopping centers.

The building of interstates has contributed to the survival and now revival of Paterson. Major roadways such as Route 46 and the Garden State Parkway have helped to make the city accessible from other parts of the county and state. Most recently, Route 80 provided a fast and easy link with New York City.

Ease of transportation between towns in the county was partly responsible for the mid-twentieth century economic decline of the urban centers. In the late twentieth century, it is assisting in the revitalization of those centers.

Paterson's Main Street Bridge is pictured in the 1860s. Courtesy, The Paterson Museum

Chapter VIII

The Twentieth Century

In November 1986 Paterson marked its 195th anniversary. The city and Passaic County through two centuries had coped with economic and natural disasters. But as the twentieth century opened, Passaic County was enjoying prosperity. In the northern parts of the county, life continued quietly, with many residents involved in either mining or farming. The cities were expanding as industry grew. Paterson was the fifteenth largest city in the nation. But the twentieth century would not be very old before the resilience displayed by Paterson and Passaic's residents would be called on again.

On the night of February 8, 1902, a fire began between Broadway and Van Houten streets in a building used to house railway cars. Wind drove the fire rapidly to surrounding buildings and despite the efforts of the Paterson Fire Department and those of nearby communities, a huge number of businesses and residences were wiped out. The devastated area ran across the city's central area, with City Hall, gutted but still standing, almost at the center of the burned section. Pictures taken at the time showed an area that resembled the aftermath of a World War II bombing raid. Between Market and Van Houten streets, from the starting point of the fire up to St. Joseph's Roman Catholic Church (corner of Market and Carroll streets), and in some places extending across these boundaries, the fire left very little standing. Remarkably, only one person was killed. Hundreds of families were homeless, and the damage totalled ten million dollars. The entire commercial hub of Paterson—banks, insurance companies, and scores of other businesses—was destroyed.

A second form of disaster struck when the Passaic River, which had contributed so much to the establishment and growth of Paterson, flooded less than four weeks later. An early thaw and heavy rainfall had led to the flooding that destroyed homes, businesses, roads, and bridges. Six people were killed. Two years later, in October 1903, still another rainfall again set off destructive flooding. These floods were but the first in a series which have plagued Passaic County throughout the years. A major flood in 1936 prompted a study of the Passaic River Basin, but it took still another flood in 1945 before the Passaic County Flood Control Commission was created. The river flooded most recently in 1984, causing millions of dollars of damage.

Paterson survived all of these early adversities and each time rebuilt. By 1910 the county was experiencing unprecedented

Facing page: Around 1900 the Paterson Washing Company, with a plant on Putnam Street, picked up, washed, and delivered laundry anywhere in the city for only fifty cents. The company only used white horses. Courtesy, Passaic County Historical Society

The first decade of this century put Paterson to the test —fires, floods, and storms rearranged the town's geography. Here, in 1903, a cyclone tore through town—while people were cleaning up from the previous year's flood. Courtesy, Passaic County Historical Society

Bad floods were once common on the Passaic River, as this photo of Main Street, north from Bank Street during the 1902 flood, demonstrates. Courtesy, Passaic County Historical Society

growth and prosperity. About 40,000 operatives were employed in manufacturing, 25,000 of which worked in the several hundred silk plants. In 1909 the Board of Trade had counted 538 establishments making products totalling close to sixty million dollars. Not only manufacturing, but professions were thriving as well, with the area providing enough business to support 140 real estate agents, 138 physicians, 130 lawyers, and twenty-two architects. Nine financial institutions took care of residents' monetary needs and several newspapers, including the *Morning Call*, *Guardian*, *Press-Chronicle* and *Evening News* kept the inhabitants informed.

There was enough prosperity among the residents of the area to support many retail establishments and travelers could choose between two hotels. There were even establishments for relaxation and physical therapy. The Broadway Bath Emporium advertised "Turkish, Russian, or Roman baths" and one entrepreneur offered the use of static electricity for those requiring "special electric treatment."

The Freeman Hotel on the corner of Ellison and Church streets offered forty-three sleeping rooms at a regular rate of one dollar and up per night or a special weekly rate starting at three dollars. The hotel featured steam heat and electric lights. The

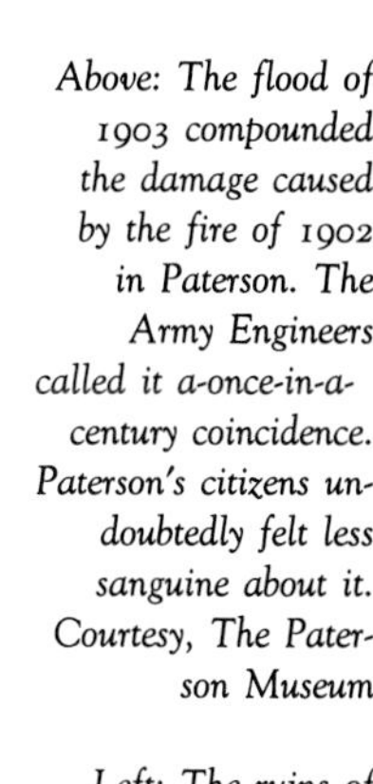

Above: The flood of 1903 compounded the damage caused by the fire of 1902 in Paterson. The Army Engineers called it a-once-in-a-century coincidence. Paterson's citizens undoubtedly felt less sanguine about it. Courtesy, The Paterson Museum

Left: The ruins of the First National Bank were photographed after the fire of 1902. The fire began in a car barn and smoldered its way through the city. Courtesy, The Paterson Museum

These silk workers were photographed for a company public relations book in about 1900. The placid scene belies the underlying problems that were to break out into open hostility a few years later. Courtesy, Passaic County Historical Society

Above: William H. McNeill posed for this photo in 1911 at his pharmacy at Straight and River streets in Paterson. The building was later an Atlantic service station. McNeill was president emeritus of the New Jersey Pharmaceutical Association. Courtesy, Passaic County Historical Society

Left: This is the city room of the Paterson Evening News in the 1920s. It does not look like the madhouse newspaper office most people perceive these days. Courtesy, Passaic County Historical Society

Right: Allen's hardware store was located on River Street in about 1920. The local beat cop stands in front of a small lumber supply yard. Courtesy, Passaic County Historical Society

Below: Before refrigerators were common, ice came from huge storage sheds like these at Hoxsey's Ice House. The ice was cut from a nearby pond and stored on racks in sheds insulated with sawdust and cork. Courtesy, Passaic County Historical Society

Bellevue Hotel on Market Street offered a bar as well as thirty-two guest rooms.

The Alexander Hamilton Hotel opened in 1924 amid great celebration. A parade to the hotel preceded dining and dancing in the elegant Grand Ballroom. The opening was organized around a theme of paying tribute to the hotel's namesake, Alexander Hamilton.

For clothing and household needs there was Meyer Brothers Department Store. It boasted five floors (not counting the basement) that could be accessed by four elevators. At least 725 employees worked in the seventy-five departments during most of the year, with 200 more added during the holiday season. One of the store's newest features was a pneumatic tube system. Meyer Brothers' main competition came from Quackenbush, which offered four floors of merchandise. The two stores carried on a Macy's and Gimbel's sort of rivalry until well into the twentieth century. Also meeting the needs of the

Alfonso Torre's fruit and vegetable shop at 43 Cross Street was photographed in the 1920s. Alfonso stands in the doorway with his children, Mildred and Arthur. His wife, Mary, is in the window at right by the coffee grinder. They are the maternal grandparents of Edward A. Smyk, Passaic County historian. Courtesy, Passaic County Historical Society

By the turn of the century, machines were replacing hand labor to cut ice at Hoxsey's Ice House. Courtesy, Passaic County Historical Society

Around 1900, this was the chief bottle washer and sorter of the David Boyle Lager Beer Company of Paterson. Courtesy, Passaic County Historical Society

Above: This 200-inch telescope disc, made by Corning Glass Works, was loaded onto a special rail car with a well-hole in preparation for a cross-country trip to the Mount Palomar Observatory. Courtesy, Passaic County Historical Society

Left: Popular Science of June 1934 published this drawing by B.G. Seiwtad of the casting process for the 200-inch Mount Palomar Observatory reflecting telescope. Produced by Corning Glass at its operations in Paterson, the scope was delivered in 1934. Courtesy, Passaic County Historical Society

The company picnic is an American tradition. This is the fourteenth annual picnic of Braun's Brewery employees, held on September 24, 1908. Courtesy, Passaic County Historical Society

citizenry were Barth's Store for men, boys, and children; S. Strum and Company for women's apparel; Miss S.M. Wells' Millinery, and Mr. Dove's Famous Cloak Store. Kitany's, The New York Furniture Store, and J. Spitz and Sons sold furnishings for homes. The Howe Motor Company, specializing in Premier and Reo automobiles, dealt in sales and service. On Market Street, F. Groten introduced a special scalp treatment whereby he found a commercial and profitable use for the then novel electricity. Pharmacies selling wares including snuff and stained glass were plentiful, as were lunch counters and restaurants. Underwood Typewriter and National Cash Register had outlets in the downtown area catering to offices and retail businesses. A variation on the "five and dime," a Three, Nine, and Nineteen Cent Store on Main Avenue presumably sold goods for these prices.

And not just business was thriving. The citizens of Passaic County could enjoy many leisure time activities. Fifty-nine social clubs and 407 societies provided diversion for everyone. Among those still in existence are the Hamilton Club, a business and social organization; the Knights of Columbus; and service clubs including the Rotary, Elks, and Masons. The PICA Club for journalists was also active. The public library, the first free public library in the state, was another source of diversion. Sports fans could watch Clifton's semi-professional baseball team, the Silk Sox, who sometimes played exhibition games with the New York Giants and Yankees.

Passaic, too, was experiencing growing prosperity at the time, ranking high among the nation's cities in production of a variety of goods. Many types of fabrics, rubber products, chemicals, and paper were turned out by Passaic factories, located mostly in the eastern part of the city. Passaic was served by three railroads; the Erie, running sixty trains daily, the Susquehanna, and the Boonton branch of the Delaware, Lacka-

Left: Fraternal organizations have always been popular in the area. This is the first annual beefsteak dinner of the Mecca Club of the Colt Association, as photographed by Heinrich's Studios. Courtesy, The Paterson Museum

Below: The annual banquet of the Paterson Grocers' Association was held at the Hamilton Hotel on Wednesday, April 7, 1937. Courtesy, Passaic County Historical Society

Facing page: This unknown, but obviously not unsung trio of amateurs, came from one of the many businessmen's clubs and YMCAs in the Paterson area around 1910. Courtesy, Passaic County Historical Society

wanna, and Western Railroad.

One endeavor not commonly associated with the area was wine-making, but the Speer New Jersey Wine Company maintained fifty acres of vineyards on Paulison and Van Houten avenues. The company made brandy, sherry, claret, and burgundy and had as much as 150,000 gallons of wine in stock at one time.

At the opposite end of the spectrum from the wealth of "Silk Baron" Catholina Lambert was the poverty of the mill workers who worked long hours in terrible factory conditions for what was barely subsistence pay. As industry grew and competition increased, mill owners pushed the workers harder, until in 1913, wages were reduced and weavers were coaxed to double the number of looms each one operated. The time was ripe for labor unrest, and Passaic was soon to become the center of such activity. Organization of workers had actually begun many years earlier, in 1879, when Joseph McDonnel founded the New Jersey Federation of Trade and Labor Unions in Paterson. In those early years, socialism was a bit too radical for the workers, and membership was small. This organization was also illegal then, as workers did not have the right to organize in New Jersey until 1883, but the foundation was being laid for upheaval. By 1900, 137 strikes had already taken place in the city. The Industrial Workers of the World leaders were interested in organizing the workers for political reasons. Some of the workers were in sympathy with the organization's political goals, while some simply were interested in more bearable conditions. The hours during each day of the six day week were long, and many modern sanitary and safety measures were unknown. Women and children, as well as men, worked long and hard in the factories.

A more major action came in 1913 at a time when the Industrial Workers of the World, the "Wobblies," were making active attempts at organizing the Paterson

One of many organizations in the colorful labor history of Paterson and Passaic County, Local 248 of the American Federation of Mechanics was photographed outside its hall between 1900 and 1910. Courtesy, Passaic County Historical Society

The Botto House was an important rallying point for the leaders of the 1913 silk strike in Paterson. Now the American Labor Museum, the house once hosted such national labor greats as Eugene V. Debs and Emma Goldman. Courtesy, Vincent Marchese

Silk strikers turned out in force in this 1913 photograph. Scenes such as this one caused unrest among Patersonians. Courtesy, Passaic County Historical Society

workers. The IWW, which had been active in another mill town, Lawrence, Massachusetts, probably saw Paterson as a likely location for labor action because of its potential value in educating the workers to revolutionary unionism and because of the miserable conditions most of the workers endured.

Conditions had been unlivable for most of the mill workers before the strike; during the strike they became much worse. The situation became so extreme, with food running short, that most of the children were sent out of the city. The propaganda value of this move was not lost on the strike organizers who widely publicized the suffering endured by the strikers.

While the "Wobblies" were active in Paterson, they established their headquarters at the Nag's Head Bar on the corner of Van Houten and Cianci streets, which is now the Question Mark Bar.

Attempting to defy the picketers and enter the mills was a dangerous endeavor. Violence broke out on many occasions. When non-striking workers tried to cross picket lines they were open to attack. Mill owners brought in outside strikebreakers who clashed with outside strike leaders brought to Paterson by the IWW. Contemporary reports described the police as being in sympathy with the mill owners, not the workers. In trying to keep control of the crowds, police battled the picketers.

The first group to strike numbered 8,000. Others joined them until in February 1913 a total of 24,000 silk and dye workers stopped work. Most of the prominent Socialists of the time and the labor movement's leaders such as William "Big Bill" Haywood, Carlo Tresca, Emma Goldman, and Eugene V. Debs all came to Paterson.

A gathering point for the strikers and their leaders was the Botto House in Haledon, now the American Labor Museum. Pietro Botto and his wife, Maria, were Italian immigrants who had worked in the mills for fifteen years, until they were able to fulfill a goal of owning their own home and garden. They shared these with other immigrants from their district in Italy who gathered at their home for socializing and recreation on weekends, as they had since

During World War I, Passaic County industry profited from more than fabrics. These three munitions factory workmen mount fuses on cannon shells. Courtesy, Passaic County Historical Society

A retired silk worker, photographed around 1930, could look forward to less-than-luxurious accommodations. The comforts of home are makeshift—the Sunday comics are a tablecloth, and despite the date he uses an oil lamp. Courtesy, The Paterson Museum

1908, when the house was built. When the workers were forbidden from gathering in Paterson, Pietro Botto permitted the use of his house as a meeting site for massive rallies. Novelist Upton Sinclair was among the well-known Socialist figures who spoke from the Botto's second floor balcony to the crowds of up to 20,000 strikers gathered in the street below. The mayor of Haledon, William Brueckmann, a Socialist who sympathized with the workers, also spoke.

For twenty-two weeks labor and management were at a stalemate. Finally, some of the workers broke ranks and began to return to the mills, and when this occurred, the unity of the IWW was lost and the strike collapsed.

As it had in the face of other problems, Paterson, with its expected resilience, bounced back again. During World War I the number of silk companies almost doubled. In 1923 the Paterson *Press-Guardian* published *Paterson in Pictures*, outlining Paterson's history and describing the city at the time. In all, 1,200 manufacturing organizations were counted, employing 50,000 people with annual wages of thirty-nine million dollars. The total value of annual production came to $225 million. Paterson had grown in spite of the strike. The silk industry itself showed growth, as 30,000 of the city's employees were involved in some phase of silk production or dyeing.

Then, in 1926, a major textile strike affected the mills of Passaic and Clifton and disrupted activity in Haledon, particularly after the workers were forbidden from holding meetings within the cities of Passaic and Clifton.

The strike began with the workers in the Botany Worsted Mill in Passaic in January 1926. Initially the strike involved woolen workers, but soon those employed in other textile mills joined. By the end of March, 16,000 employees were on strike. The Passaic Worsted Mill, Gera Mills, Forstmann and Huffman, Dundee Textile and United Piece Dye Works were affected. This strike, like the one of 1913, had been triggered by a wage cut. The workers' demands included a retraction of the wage cut, a 10 percent increase over the old wages, time and a half for overtime, a forty-hour week, improved working conditions, and recognition of the union.

The United Front Committee, under the

Above: These silkworkers' homes are seen in pre-Depression Paterson when times were good. Courtesy, The Paterson Museum

Left: During the Great Depression, shanty towns like this could be found in Passaic County. Courtesy, The Paterson Museum

Manchester School No. 11 at Goffle Hill Road, Hawthorne, New Jersey, was photographed by Walter A. Lucas in 1934. Courtesy, Passaic County Historical Society

direction of Albert Weisbord, was organizing the picket line and arranging for support of the strikers and their families. Some strikers were sent to Washington to picket the White House. Organizers used the strike as an example of action the rest of the country's workers should be taking to end their own exploitation. The strike was well covered by the local press, the New York press, and the wire services.

As the strike of 1913 helped to put an end to the dominance of the silk industry in Paterson, the 1926 Passaic textile strike had much the same effect on the textile industries, although since large mills were struck, they were better equipped to survive. There was another side of life in Passaic County in the early twentieth century, the rural side. It was described by Hester MacDonald Cappio in *Life on a Valley Road Farm*. She had grown up on a truck farm on Valley Road in Preakness and described an existence quite different from that of the urban mill workers. As a child, her time was spent doing farm chores such as feeding the family's chickens or gathering nuts with a group of friends. Playtime was easily filled with horseback riding, tree climbing, ice skating, picking flowers, or pitching horseshoes. The MacDonald family farm grew a variety of crops, including potatoes, corn, tomatoes, cabbage, peppers, egg plant, beets, carrots, and hay. The MacDonalds also maintained an apple orchard, cattle, and horses, and a spring on the property provided drinking water.

Clifton, too, was largely farmland until 1940, when it was developed as a suburb. Following the trend of the times, it soon exceeded more urban Passaic in population.

In the 1980s one of the most active industries in the county is health care. The area's health requirements are met by a number of hospitals. In Paterson, Barnert Memorial was founded in 1908 to help serve the immigrants. It is named for Nathan Barnert, the philanthropist who founded the hospital, which recently completed a major expansion program. Passaic General Hospital and Paterson General, originally "Ladies Hospital" in Wayne, offer many services to in-and-out patients.

St. Joseph's Hospital was founded in 1867 by Father McNulty and five Sisters of Charity. Paterson's first hospital, it is now one of the largest in New Jersey, admitting more than 20,000 patients per year as well as offering outpatient services to more than 100,000. Beginning with twelve beds and growing to the present count of 530, St. Joseph's has remained dedicated to serving those unable to pay. And it has found

Shown here is the Passaic County Medical Society at its May 12, 1938, meeting. Courtesy, Passaic County Historical Society

creative solutions to its problems. Sister Jane Frances Brady recently described the juggling of available funds that took place as recently as the 1970s to keep the hospital financially afloat. In order to remain in a position to care for the poor, the hospital became a regionally designated hospital for several services including prenatal care, newborn intensive care, and other specialties such as cardiology and psychiatry. Brady pointed out that in addition to the hospital providing these services and cutting down on travel for patients nearby, the income generated through these specialties allows the hospital to continue treating members of the community unable to pay.

World War II brought a certain degree of prosperity to Paterson through a new activity, jet engine building. In this instance, Paterson's typical dependence on one or two industries narrowed to dependence on a single company, but one that, at its highest production, used as much space in its plant on Beckwith Avenue as all the locomotive building companies had used at their peak production. Orville and Wilbur Wright had founded the Dayton-Wright Company which was taken over by the Wright-Martin Company of New Brunswick in 1916. In 1919 the company reorganized and moved to Paterson as the Wright Aeronautical Corporation. Glenn Curtiss, who had developed a business first by building bicycle engines, later dirigible engines, and eventually planes, merged his company with Wright in 1929 to become Curtiss-Wright. The company grew from an early count of 350 employees to tens of thousands. The growth of the company was aided by a marketing dream; Charles Lindbergh's plane, *The Spirit of St. Louis,* was powered by a Wright Whirlwind engine. Amelia Earhart made the first crossing of the Atlantic by a woman in a plane powered by a Wright engine.

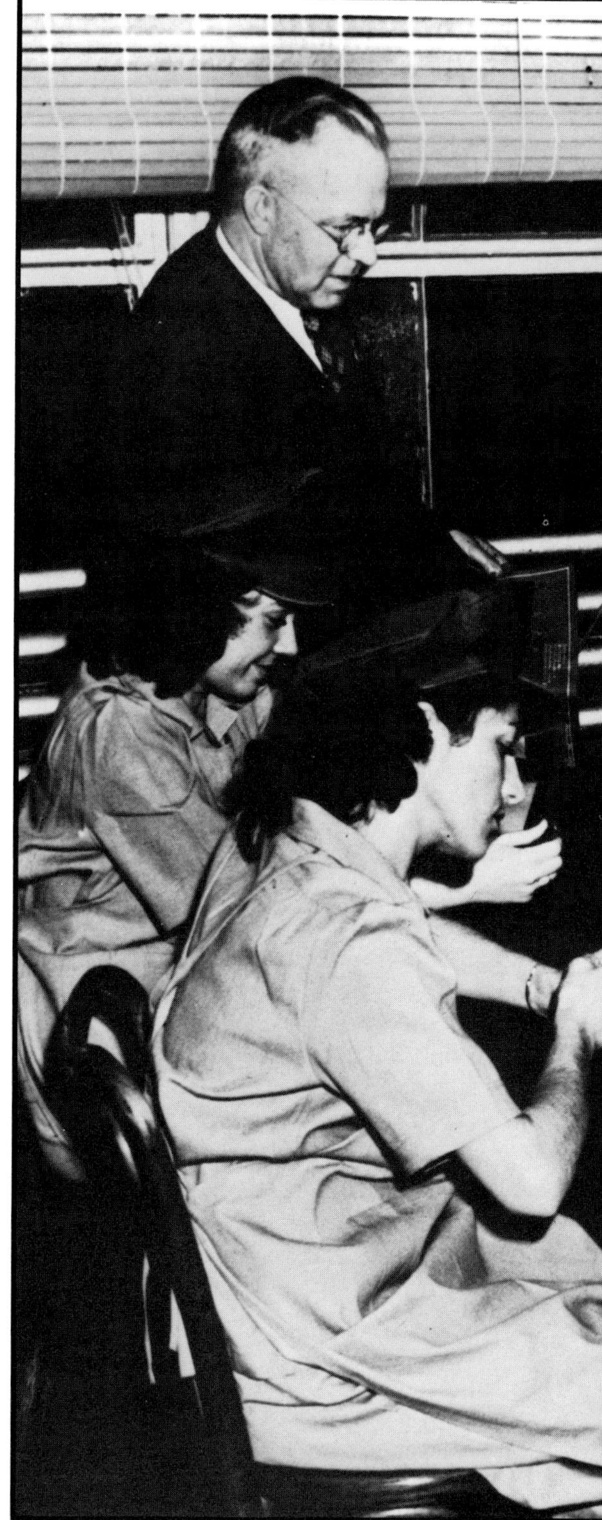

Curtiss-Wright played a vital role during World War II by building engines that powered some of the United States' most

To help with the war effort early in 1942, women received special training to assemble military equipment. Courtesy, Passaic County Historical Society

The Paterson Red Cross ambulance is shown in about 1920. Courtesy, Passaic County Historical Society

famous planes, including the B-17 Flying Fortress, the B-29 Super Fortress, the planes used in bombing Hiroshima and Nagasaki, the B-25 used in the first American bombing raid on Tokyo, and the DC-3. Between 1941 and 1945 Curtiss-Wright employed almost 50,000 workers and produced 139,000 engines. Employees worked three shifts, turning out three engines an hour at the peak of the war. The average worker made less than one dollar per hour. The growth of commercial passenger flight following World War II continued the demand for engines. Lockheed *Constellations* and *Electras*, Boeing-*Stratoliners*, and *Clippers* all used Curtiss-Wright engines. The company's engines powered the first transatlantic flight in 1939, the first commercial round-the-world flight in 1947, Pan Am's first passenger flight in 1928, and the first flight from the United States to Asia in 1936. Admiral Richard Byrd flew to the North Pole using the Wright engine. The company not only pioneered mass production of jet engines but manufactured engines used in tanks, helicopters, and gun carriers. The company made jet engines to help power space rockets. A recent new peacetime use has been discovered for the turbo jet engine: it can cool and mix air and water, which when atomized and sprayed into the atmosphere at freezing temperatures, makes snow. Many of the engines, including ten restored by two former Wright employees, George Abbamont and Andrew W. Smith, are on display at The Paterson Museum.

In spite of the success of the Curtiss-Wright Company, Paterson's decline continued after World War II, especially after the company moved its plant to Woodbridge. The company stopped building engines completely in 1982. For textile companies, labor was cheaper in the south, where there was room and inspiration to build modern plants. The older mills and factories in Passaic and Paterson were abandoned as textile industries moved south. While many of the suburban communities enjoyed a postwar building boom, the cities plummeted downhill. The suburbs were becoming self-supporting; employment was available in industries that had built in the less expensive and more readily available land in the suburbs and provided local employment; and the growth of malls and centers allowed shopping for most products without having to travel to a downtown city area.

Although Paterson felt the effects of some of the turbulence of the 1960s, including a sit-in for civil rights at City Hall, it escaped the major race riots that devastated other northern New Jersey industrial cities such as Newark and Elizabeth. In part, this was managed through cooperation between minority community leaders and members of the city administration, and in part through creativity. Stories are told of mayor Lawrence "Pat" Kramer, who convinced bands to play in the streets of potentially explosive sections of the city so that the young people most likely to rampage would channel their energy into dancing rather than destruction.

In spite of the decline, Paterson remained important enough to have been a campaign stop for John F. Kennedy, Dwight D. Eisenhower, and Adlai Stevenson. Martin Luther King, too, spoke to more than capacity crowds a few days before his death in 1968. President Ronald Reagan stopped in Paterson during the 1980 presidential campaign. Other political figures who visited the city included Wendell L. Wilkie, Al Smith, and Eleanor Roosevelt.

The 1970s saw a continued decline in prosperity, with few people and industries moving into the city and many moving out into the suburbs. It was during this decade, though, that the foundation for a new realization of both the significance of the city's past and its future potential was blueprinted. Developments in the 1980s, many of them based on the past, contain promise for the future.

Chapter IX

299

Past as Prologue

Passaic County is today experiencing an awakening of interest in its past. This attention to yesterday is leading to a renewal, particularly of Paterson. Exploring the past is one of the aspects drawing people to Paterson. As the county celebrates its 150th anniversary, it presents a valuable microcosm of industrial America and the immigrant experience in the industrial cities. It also suggests a revitalization of a community that offers much of which to be proud. Many new people are attracted by the advantages of city living—in terms of cost and location. People whose families had been from Paterson but who had left the city are discovering the advantages of an urban setting—close to the hustle and bustle of New York City, yet but a short drive to the almost 600 acres of Garrett Mountain Reservation.

Much of the current fascination with the past stems from an effort to save the mills and associated buildings from being razed in the face of highway construction. Mary Ellen Kramer, wife of Pat Kramer, former mayor of Paterson, and John Young, a graduate student in architecture, have led a group interested in saving the buildings. In 1971 the Great Falls Development Corporation was founded to further not only preservation but restoration of the section. Factory buildings and mills have been restored and they now house businesses, offices, artists' studios, apartments, and a school. Restored streetlights and signs reinforce a feel of the past in a 119-acre area. In 1976 President Gerald Ford visited Paterson to designate the falls and its surrounding area as a National Historic Landmark, thus citing Paterson's importance in determining the nation's industrial direction.

Another demonstration of interest is in the efforts of Derek Moore, a resident of Macclesfield, England, who currently is trying to put workers who emigrated to Paterson, or their descendents, in touch with one another.

Passaic County's population has grown by approximately 41,000 in the past twenty-five years, with Paterson's population of almost 140,000 accounting for about one-third of the county's total. After being identified in 1981 as "one of the most distressed cities on the mainland of America," according to Mayor Francis X. Graves, it has in the past five years served as a site of major construction and renewal. Businesses have been attracted to Paterson by the available space and labor pool and its access to transportation. The population

Facing page: This Rogers 2-6-4 locomotive is now on display at The Paterson Museum. Courtesy, Vincent Marchese

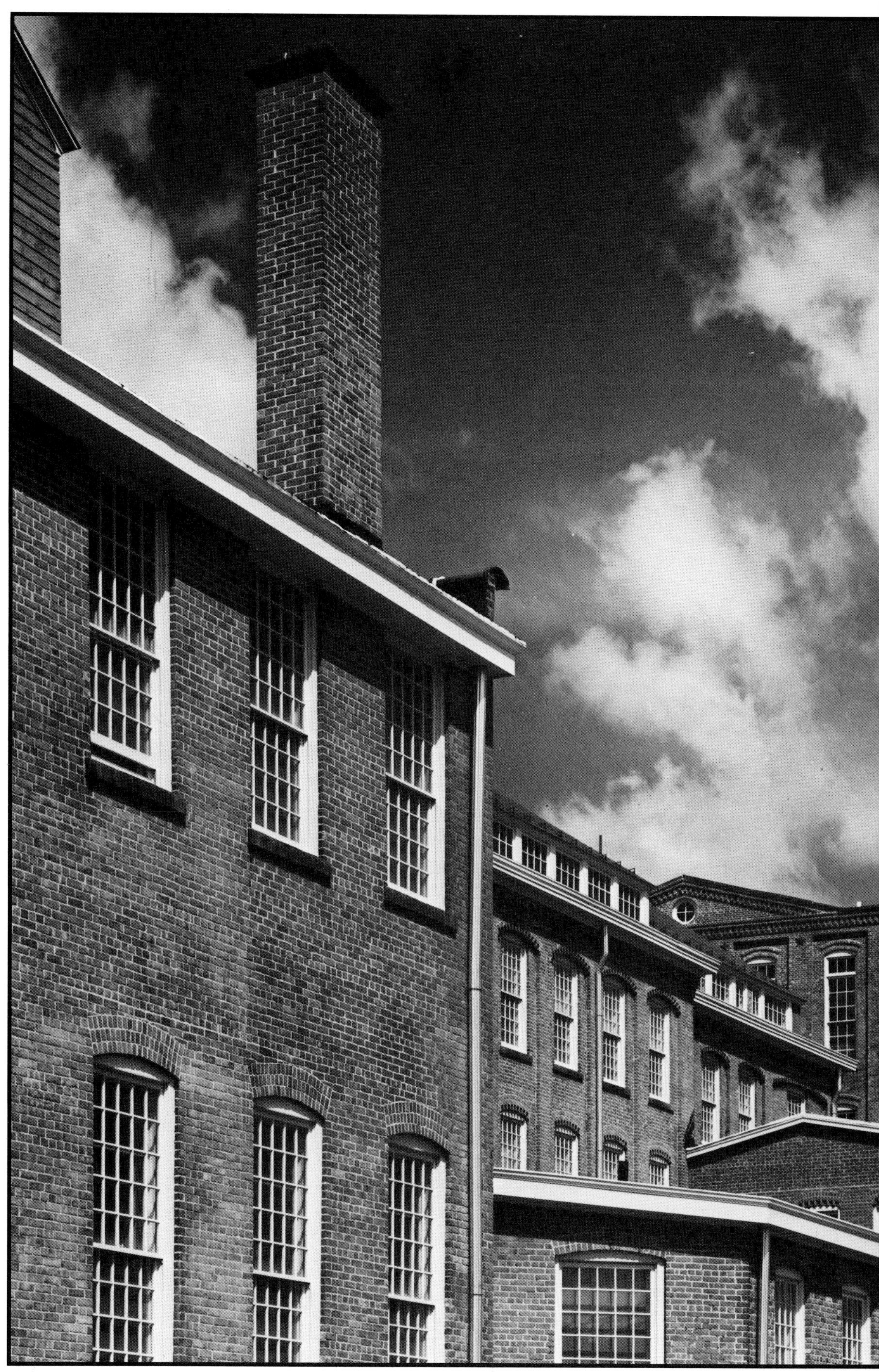

The old Rogers Building, which once housed a foundry and shops, is now the site of The Paterson Museum. The museum maintains permanent and featured exhibits which deal with Paterson's industrial past. Courtesy, Vincent Marchese

The Paterson Public Library was located in the Danforth house. The picture was taken before a fire necessitated building the present Danforth Memorial Library. Courtesy, Passaic County Historical Society

that had been leaving the city is staying or returning, sometimes initially drawn by the city's restoration and history and staying because of the low real estate prices. In West Paterson, a 350-unit condominium development is being constructed. The Paterson east side, with its many Victorian mansions, has remained fashionable.

Some of the newest residents are continuing, on a smaller basis, the activities that gave Paterson its glory days—by establishing many small machine shops and cloth and garment businesses. In June of 1986 the *New York Times* reported that the French workers who crafted the new flame for the rededication of the Statue of Liberty have opened a shop in Paterson. Another Statue of Liberty-connected company, the Jane Street Corporation, manufactured elevator doors for the statue.

Landmarks outside the district have also been recognized for their historic value. The Danforth Memorial Library has been added to the National Register of Historic Places. The building was designed by Henry Bacon, designer of the Lincoln Memorial in Washington, D.C. A major contributor to the library's building fund, Mrs. William Ryle requested that the library be named for her father, Charles Danforth. The building features names of philosophers and authors carved into its exterior.

In 1982 the American Labor Museum purchased the Botto House in Haledon, site of rallies during the 1913 and 1926 strikes, and established a museum there honoring the American worker. This house also has been listed in the National Register of Historic Places.

John Holland's submarine, tested in the Passaic River, was the predecessor of all modern Navy submarines. The first class of United States Navy submarines was known as the "Holland Class" after a later submarine designed by Holland became the first commissioned submarine in the Navy

in 1900. For ease of viewing and its protection, this vessel, the *Fenian Ram*, was moved with appropriate ceremony, including the Naval Academy Drum and Bugle Corps and the Navy Glee Club, from Westside Park to the museum in Rogers Locomotive Works.

Many works of noted sculptor Gaetano Federici can be viewed in Paterson, including his *Spring No More* in the Dublin section. A monument to honor the Reverend William McNulty, rector of St. John's Cathedral from 1863 to 1922, can be seen outside the church at Grand Street.

Federici statues outside City Hall honor two of Paterson's notable statesmen. One, of Nathan Barnert, a philanthropist and two-time mayor of Paterson, was finished in 1925, and another of Andrew F. McBride, M.D., who served three terms as mayor of the city, was completed in 1947. A third statue, depicting Garrett A. Hobart, also stands in front of City Hall. It was sculpted by Philip Martiny in 1902.

Other monuments include the veterans' memorial in Eastside Park and the statue of Alexander Hamilton by Franklin Simmons that appropriately overlooks the falls. Several buildings outside the Historic District in Paterson have been noted as outstanding examples of different types of architecture: City Hall and the L'Enfant Building as Beaux Arts; the old courthouse as classical; the old post office, at present an annex to the courthouse as Flemish Renaissance, and John Ryle's house as Greek Revival.

Scordato's restaurant advertises its present location (since 1970) as being in the former DeGray home. Built in 1730, it was once owned by John Francis Ryerson, and Lafayette's light infantry camped in there 1780. Some of the original building remains on Wagaraw road.

The number of buildings, streets, and institutions named for some of the historic figures in the county's past serve as reminders. For instance, the name "Hamilton" alone has been used for a street, a bank, and a building.

The county has produced its share of notables who have contributed in a variety of fields including art, sports, medicine, government, and entertainment. Author Albert Payson Terhune used his home in Pompton Lakes, Sunnybank, as the setting for his stories about a series of dogs bred at the kennel there. Terhune first became known as a newspaper columnist, but it was the stories about "Lad" and other dogs that brought him success and fame. A childhood resident of Pompton Lakes, Cecil B. DeMille, grew up to direct epic films. DeMille's family attended services at Pompton Christ Church. Garrett A. Hobart, a native of Paterson, was chosen on the first ballot at the 1896 Republican Convention to be William McKinley's running mate and was subsequently elected vice president. He also served in the United States Senate, but before that, he was speaker of the New Jersey Assembly and president of the New Jersey Senate.

A somewhat less-known figure is Sam Patch, a former mill worker from Paterson, who during his heyday was widely celebrated for an unusual talent in leaping from high places and surviving. Patch made an unexpected jump at the dedication of the first bridge over the falls in 1827, thus launching his career, which in 1829 included a successful leap over Niagara Falls.

Allen Ginsberg, who grew up in Paterson and has used the city as a subject for several poems, was recently honored at the William Carlos Williams Poetry Festival.

Two Paterson residents who have recently gained prominence in government are Alfred Kahn, who served as the head of President Jimmy Carter's anti-inflation program, and William E. Simon, secretary of the treasury under former President Richard M. Nixon.

Paterson residents who made significant advances in medicine include Albert Sabin, who developed the oral polio vaccine, and

Facing page: The courtyard at Ringwood Manor depicts what its early owners believed to be simple country elegance. Courtesy, Vincent Marchese

Golden-orange trees highlight the beauty of Ringwood Manor State Park in autumn. Courtesy, Vincent Marchese

Saul Krugman, who invented innoculations for hepatitis and rubella.

Actress Loretta Swit, United States Senator Frank Lautenberg, the first black baseball player in the American League Larry Doby, and comedian Lou Costello, who greeted "all the folks out in Paterson" during his broadcasts, are all natives of Passaic County.

Mayor Frank Graves and Greater Paterson Chamber of Commerce President Vincent J. Cortese both have cited cooperation between public and private sectors as a factor largely responsible for the city's rejuvenation. Construction has been increasing tremendously in recent years, amounting to $150,000 in 1986.

Both St. Joseph's and St. Barnert's hospitals are undergoing major expansion programs. Barnert is completing a thirty-nine-million-dollar expansion program and St. Joseph's an eighty-million-dollar program.

One of Paterson's strengths is its diversity of population—approximately 37 percent are white, 34 percent are black and 27 percent are Hispanic. In the early decades of the twentieth century the recently arrived immigrants were mostly Irish, Italian, or German; the newest residents are now Arabic, Korean, Chilean, Dominican, Puerto Rican, Vietnamese, or Mexican. Sister Jane Frances Brady of St. Joseph's points out that although this is a new group ethnically, many of the problems for the poorer newcomers haven't changed. Poverty still keeps the tuberculosis rate for the city much higher than the national average and while some of the problems brought on by poverty have been alleviated, new ones have taken their place.

Urban problems remain. The plight of the homeless was underlined as recently as October 18, 1984, by a fire in the once lavish Alexander Hamilton Hotel, leaving 300 welfare recipients homeless. Many adjoining businesses were also damaged. Thirteen people were killed, and fifty-nine

were injured, marking this as the worst conflagration since 1902. At least 175 firefighters fought the blaze with assistance from surrounding towns including Passaic, Clifton, Hawthorne, Prospect Park, West Paterson, and Haledon. Survivors were offered shelter at the John F. Kennedy High School, the Paterson YMCA, and Camp Hope in West Milford.

Another massive fire struck in Passaic on

During a cold winter, the spillway at Paterson can present an eerie scene. Courtesy, The Paterson Museum

Facing page: This tree-shaded home in northwest Paterson presents a perfect picture of peace and quiet. Photo by Bill Croul

September 2, 1985. A four-block industrial section on Eighth Street was destroyed in spite of the efforts of firefighters. One firefighter died in the blaze; 4,800 people were evacuated, and 800 were left homeless. In Passaic, the Labor Day weekend fire that destroyed Gera Mills brought attention to the Polish and Slavik immigrants still trapped by language and cultural differences, isolated in much the same way mill workers were at the beginning of the twentieth century. Many of the workers left jobless either lacked or lost documents in the fire that would allow them to seek other jobs or receive aid. These workers still lived in the section of the city traditionally populated by immigrants, named the Dundee section for the large number of Irish who once lived there.

The new diversity in business may break the cycle of depression and prosperity Paterson has experienced for most of its history. Rather than being dependent on one business or industry, there are now many. The largest single employer in the city of Paterson, St. Joseph's Hospital, employs 3,000 people.

With the renaissance of the Great Falls/SUM district has come greater effort in developing the downtown area. The economic climate of the northeast has changed. New Jersey has the lowest unemployment figures in the country. Paterson has shared that prosperity. Land values are now three to four times what they were five years ago. Industries are appearing at record rates and more growth is planned.

To address the challenges of the future, the Paterson authorities, with the aid of the Chamber of Commerce, have seen to a greater participation by minorities. The Private Industry Council (PIC) is moving Paterson forward. The PIC provides training and employment opportunities for the huge labor pool of Paterson and has been successfully developing the valuable human resources of Paterson since its inception in 1983.

The master plan is presently to keep local people doing business in Paterson and to bring in offices and service industries. The Superblock will be the keystone of this revitalization project. Superblock will be a huge, multiuse section of Paterson bounded by Ward, Clark, Main, and Market streets. Made up of three large office, retail, and residential structures and serviced by underground and above ground parking facilities, Superblock will bring in corporate headquarters that want the convenience of I-80; closeness to New York City without the high taxes, rents, and crime; and the benefits of employees living in whatever setting they choose—rural to metropolitan—without being more than a few minutes from work and recreation. The New Jersey Department of Transportation has already purchased twenty major properties that will be the site of a new I-80 ramp directly into the heart of the city.

Vincent J. Cortese has been with the Greater Paterson Chamber of Commerce for thirty years, and has seen his organization grow from 200 to 1,200 members in just twelve years. He points with pride to the fact that the development of Paterson, now in its seventh regeneration since 1792, is pulling together without regard to partisan politics, and that both government and the business community are cooperating without the acrimony of past decades. Lawrence Kramer once said of Paterson politics that, "This city doesn't need a mayor, it needs a referee." That becomes increasingly untrue as people became more "bullish" on Paterson.

The natural and human resources of Passaic County have combined to create an illustrious past. These same qualities ensure its future. The river and falls, having less influence now, remain an inspiration, and as Allen Ginsberg points out in a poem about Paterson, a constant: "Only the Great Falls and the Passaic River flow noisy with the mist and then quietly along the brick factory sides as they did before."

Right: Surrounded by trees, this home in eastern Paterson depicts stately charm. Photo by Bill Croul

Below: Proud of its past, Paterson displays this sign, designating the city's National Historic District. Photo by Bill Croul

Facing page: The old Rogers Locomotive Works now houses The Paterson Museum. Photo by Bill Croul

Left and far left: The mighty Great Falls that thunder over the Passaic River symbolize the City of Paterson's self-perpetuating power. Courtesy, New Jersey Department of Travel and Tourism

Ice sailing on Greenwood Lake is a fast and exciting winter sport. Courtesy, New Jersey Department of Travel and Tourism

These private school students quietly pursue individual interests, activities, and assignments. Photo by Bill Croul

Paterson Catholic Regional High School is shown in this Bill Croul photograph.

These folks get a bird's eye view of Paterson from their vantage point on Garrett Mountain. Photo by Bill Croul

Left: The Old County Courthouse is a striking example of classic design. Photo by Bill Croul

Far left: Built by silk baron Catholina Lambert, Belle Vista Castle on Garrett Mountain is now the home of the Passaic County Historical Society. Photo by Bill Croul

Above: The Paterson City Hall is a favorite historic landmark in the city. Photo by Bill Croul

Below: The Flemish Courthouse stands in stark contrast to the surrounding buildings. Photo by Bill Croul

Facing page: The front gate of skylands Manor is shown here. Courtesy, Vincent Marchese

Following page: In the days of steam, great sluice gates controlled water levels in the mill races of the society for Useful Manufactures. Now restored, the millraces lend tranquility to the historic area of Paterson. Courtesy, Paterson Museum

Chapter X

PUBLIC SERVICE ELECTRIC
AND GAS CO., PATERSON, N.J.

Partners in Progress

Economic life was an elemental part of the history of what are now Paterson and Passaic County long before there were maps of the area. And the Great Falls of the Passaic River flow today as they have for millennia, linking the earliest years of this land with the unknown discoveries of a century soon to be born.

Since the time of its earliest inhabitants, the Passaic Valley has served as a center of economic activity. From the hunting and fishing of native Americans to the working farms of Dutch settlers and their descendants, the region provided its inhabitants with a natural abundance.

But it was the inauguration of industry at the new nation's first manufacturing center—Paterson—that carried the force of those Great Falls to the ages that followed. That progression may have begun with a legendary picnic lunch enjoyed by young Alexander Hamilton with his commander in chief during the Revolutionary War, but history has flowed with the Passaic River for more than 200 years of this nation's life.

Paterson's cotton mills, locomotive plants producing fire-breathing behemoths that carried millions of men on both sides during the Civil War yet also were present when east was united with west at the striking of the golden spike in Utah four years after the war, and then the silk industry that gave the city a nickname it retains today are milestones on Paterson and Passaic County's historic path.

There are so many other significant moments and elements to the economic history of the city and its county—and their contributions to the development of this country—that can be cited. The Morris Canal, the trade centered around Acquackanonk Landing (today's City of Passaic), the first practical submarine, the engine that powered Lindbergh's tiny airplane across the Atlantic, the farmlands of modern Clifton and other communities that became the twentieth-century "homesteads" of GIs returning from World War II, and the outcropping of seemingly ubiquitous office developments and retail centers that occupy what was once open land are all part of the tremendous flow of history through the Passaic Valley.

Factories teeming with immigrants seeking opportunity, retail establishments serving diversified tastes and needs of local residents, chemical and pharmaceutical industries, financial institutions, professionals, and laborers all illustrate that Paterson and Passaic County have been rich in resources—human, locational, and natural—that have made the area a vibrant economic unit.

Today Paterson and Passaic County—and members of the business community that are truly "Partners in Progress"—approach the twenty first century with confidence arising from more than 200 years' experience in building on the foundations of the past.

The organizations whose stories are detailed on the following pages have chosen to support this important literary and civic project. They illustrate the variety of ways in which individuals and their businesses have contributed to the county's growth and development. The civic involvement of Passaic County's businesses, institutions of learning, and local government, in cooperation with its citizens, has made the area na excellent place to live and work.

GREATER PATERSON CHAMBER OF COMMERCE

From its founding as the Board of Trade, the Greater Paterson Chamber of Commerce has been a unifying force within the business communities of Paterson and the surrounding cities in addressing the concerns of a modern world. Since the convening of the first Board of Trade in 1908, the chamber (as it became in 1914) has served as a forum for issues affecting not only business and industrial interests, but also social, environmental, and other questions faced by all elements within the region.

The Board of Trade was a spirited group that grew from 250 charter members to more than 1,000 members in three years. Its one-room office was located in city hall.

In 1914 the organization relocated to a three-room suite in the Colt Building at the corner of Colt and Ellison streets. Its offices were later moved to various other locations until settling in the refurbished Oakley Building at 211 Market Street. It remained there until a 1962 fire destroyed the structure with the irreplaceable loss of records and historical artifacts, including the priceless Reid Collection of old Paterson photographs. The chamber then moved to 262 Main Street, followed by relocation in 1973 to its present headquarters in the city's downtown office tower at 100 Hamilton Plaza.

From the outset the chamber dealt with a broad array of concerns, many of which, such as transportation, development, and education, remain on its current agenda.

In earlier days the concern for improving transportation centered on trolley fares and the hazards of railroad grade crossings. More recently the chamber has expressed business and community views on bus routes, schedules, and fares; improving commuter and freight railway systems; and the routing and expansion of highway networks.

The chamber has always advanced local development, providing jobs, homes, and amenities of life for the people of the city and its neighbors. It spearheaded the construction of hotels, office buildings, public garages, manufacturing complexes, Hamilton Plaza, and renewal of the Great Falls Historic District.

Progressive business leaders understand that education leads to better prepared employees and managers. The chamber's advocacy of educational opportunities led to development of the Passaic County Vocational and Technical High School, maturing of the Paterson Normal School into the William Paterson State College, and, most recently, the creation of the Passaic County Community College.

The organization remains the most active group in the greater Paterson area, dealing with social and economic issues such as economic/industrial developement, governmental affairs, central business district developement, area marketing, and membership services.

Vincent J. Cortese, the chamber's chief executive since 1968, sums up the organization's role: "For nearly 80 years the Greater Paterson Chamber of Commerce has served this area. Its more than 1,300 members—representing corporations, industries, stores, service firms, utilities, financial institutions, and more—are working to make the region better in every facet: economic opportunities, culture, education, government, and ensuring a brighter future."

The staff of the Greater Paterson Chamber of Commerce (from left): Robert Kearny, secretary; Glenn F. Harvey, associate director; Vincent J. Cortese, president; Gladys Bayon, secretary/ bookkeeper; and (seated) Helen Atkins, secretary to the president and office manager.

Pictured here is a display of regional directories in the gallery of the chamber offices at 32 Church Street in 1934.

BOGRAD'S

In 1939 the Bograd Brothers, Inc., annual dinner-dance was held at the Colonial Inn.

The greatest testament to a retail establishment's success is its ability to draw customers from beyond its "normal" market area. Bograd's is such an emporium, attracting customers to Paterson from throughout North Jersey, New York City, and beyond because of its reputation for quality furniture and personal service.

Samuel and David Bograd's family was part of the flood of immigrants passing the Statue of Liberty after World War I. The Bograd boys seized the opportunities their new home offered by becoming door-to-door salesmen while still attending school.

While there were many stores in existence during the 1920s, they were often beyond the modest means of workers, especially the new Americans flocking to the factories of Paterson. Door-to-door salesmen of the day, like the Bograds, provided everything from clothing to furniture. Customers relied on the brothers for value and service, and the Bograds earned a reputation for quality and caring. Despite the uncertainty of the Depression years, the brothers mustered the courage to open a store on August 1, 1930.

The Bograd Brothers store, located at 92 Market Street, carried a diversified inventory of furniture, appliances, and even clothing. As in their selling days, the brothers built their business by serving customers' total needs. By 1935 the Bograds had outgrown the store. On the first of August, five years to the day after opening, the store was moved to 288 Main Street, where it remains today.

The U.S. entry into World War II brought changes. Shortages of goods bedeviled consumers and merchants alike. With the end of the war and the advent of the 1950s, Bograd Brothers returned to serving a broad-based clientele, especially returning servicemen equipping their new "G.I. houses" throughout North Jersey.

The market was changing. The suburbs became the focus of residential development, and thousands of families left urban centers such as Paterson. Shopping malls, located on new highways, were drawing away middle-class shoppers from Paterson and other cities' shopping areas.

Samuel and David Bograd accepted the challenge by redirecting their store's mission. They focused their inventory on items aimed at customers for whom quality was paramount. They looked beyond their traditional Paterson market, seeking customers who valued superior merchandise and service.

In the 1950s and 1960s Bograd Brothers extended its bounds by advertising in such publications as *The New York Times Magazine.* The strategy worked; today nearly 95 percent of Bograd's business comes from outside Paterson, and 40 percent comes from out of state.

In 1973 David Bograd died, ending a partnership that lasted more than 40 years. Ownership then passed to Samuel, and his son Joseph, who had joined the firm in 1956 after graduating from Cornell, assumed control of the store's day-to-day operations.

In 1979 the building next to 288 Main Street was purchased. Following renovations that joined the two structures, Bograd's opened Thanksgiving weekend in 1980, only months after the company celebrated its 50th anniversary. Featuring larger showrooms in addition to warehousing and shipping facilities, the enlarged Bograd's brought all operations under one roof for the first time in 50 years.

"Bograd Brothers began serving working people who wanted good service and value for their money," says Joseph Bograd. "Our store has emphasized quality and service for more than a half-century. We continue to play a pivotal role in maintaining the city's prominence, today and for the future."

BROADWAY BANK & TRUST COMPANY

The Broadway Bank & Trust Company building on the corner of Broadway and West Broadway after its 1956 remodeling.

When Martin Sukenick gazes out his office window, across the wide plaza lying before the 14-story office tower rising above Paterson that is the headquarters of the bank he has served for more than 40 years, there is a perceptible sense of accomplishment and satisfaction. Yet his visage also shows the restless yearning for new challenges that sets the pace for the chairman of Broadway Bank & Trust Company—and for the institution he leads. Sukenick molded the small Broadway Bank to become, with more than $270 million in assets, the largest commercial bank headquartered in Paterson, where America's second revolution, the Industrial Revolution, began nearly two centuries ago.

The city has seen many business leaders—demanding, visionary individuals—since Alexander Hamilton founded it as the nation's first industrial center. Sukenick, at the helm of Broadway Bank, shared that heritage and capitalized on it. He led his bank to its greatest growth and profitability, while achieving an unparalleled record of service to a unique city.

Established as Broadway National Bank, the institution opened its doors on November 2, 1925. Located at Broadway and Church Street, total assets amounted to nearly $400,000. By the close of business July 1, 1929, assets amounted to more than $2.3 million.

The placing of the cornerstone for the Broadway Bank building at Broadway and West Broadway on August 12, 1931. On the right (with the trowel) is John McCutchem, then bank chairman.

During that fateful year the bank experienced a change in management, with former state comptroller John McCutchem becoming chairman of the board. It was converted from a federal-chartered institution to a state-chartered bank and trust company, allowing for a broader range of services to its customers.

Despite the uncertainties of the Great Depression, Broadway Bank & Trust Company looked forward with confidence, and on August 12, 1931, laid the cornerstone for a headquarters building at the intersection of Broadway and West Broadway, near Paterson's downtown shopping area. Reflecting the retail character of the area, the first floor of the building housed seven stores with banking quarters located on the second floor.

Broadway Bank & Trust Company's resources stood at nearly $1.8 million in January 1933. On March 16, 1933, following the nationwide Bank Holiday, the institution reopened and within two years had qualified for F.D.I.C. insurance, then covering individual deposits of up to $5,000.

Through the 1930s and into the war years of the early 1940s, Broadway Bank continued to strengthen its financial position and status as an involved community institution. In 1942 Nathaniel Kent, a highly respected local attorney and counsel to the bank, became chairman of the board, with George W. Renkel as president. Following the war Martin Sukenick joined the bank, which then had eight million dollars in deposits.

The postwar years were extraordinarily active for the institution. Broadway Bank & Trust became the leading originator of G.I. mortgages and generated some $85 million in home financings throughout North Jersey. Putting that figure in perspective, during the late 1940s and 1950s the average mortgage loan was only $10,000.

Dealing with such a volume of loans was ideal for Sukenick. An accountant by profession, he applied his knowledge of automated techniques, learned in the military, to servicing thousands of mortgages. That experience led to Broadway Bank's successful introduction of the computer to New Jersey's banking industry in the early 1950s; it was one of only 14 banks nationwide to install a computer at the time.

While Broadway Bank & Trust Company did not seek to be the largest bank in the greater Paterson area, it did strive to be innovative. In addition to electronic data processing during the 1950s, the institution initiated other steps, including selling mortgages to the secondary market which freed up funds for reinvestment while earning the bank servicing fees (for which the computer was a major cost-saving benefit).

In addition, the bank began financing insurance premiums inside and outside New Jersey. It also became a leading Small Business Administration lender to new and growing companies. And, going into the 1960s, the institution became prominent in assisting black and other minority-owned businesses in Paterson.

Martin Sukenick (left), chairman of the board, and Peter M. Kolben, bank president.

The essence of banking today, says Sukenick, is accepting change and being willing to experiment with new service products and to open new markets, such as that of the minority community. "If you don't change, you die," he says. "Paterson was changing and so was all of North Jersey. If we couldn't alter the course of this city economically and socially, the bank would have died."

Broadway Bank & Trust Company became deeply involved in community relations programs in Paterson, fostering new lines of communications in the city and taking a direct role in developing the city's potential, such as the historic Great Falls District. When Canal-Randolph Development Corporation proposed a modern office tower for downtown Paterson, it was appropriate that Broadway Bank chose that structure to house its new corporate headquarters, occupied in 1974.

While the bank tended to its roots in Paterson, it also embarked on a program of controlled expansion into other regions in the late 1960s and 1970s. The institution's first suburban banking center was opened in Pompton Plains in 1969. Today Broadway Bank offices are found in Fairfield, Kinnelon, Midland Park, Montvale, Park Ridge, Little Falls, Teaneck, and Wayne.

The 1970s and 1980s saw the entire banking industry undergo deregulation, allowing banks to broaden their service bases while increasing competition both from other banks and from nonbanking sources. Discount brokerage, expanded electronic information services, new depository instruments such as money market accounts, innovative credit products, and other opportunities are posing additional challenges to Broadway Bank & Trust Company, as well as other financial services providers.

Recognizing the need for new leadership for a future of increased competition, Broadway Bank & Trust Company elected Peter M. Kolben as president in 1978. The institution formed its own holding company, Broadway Financial Corporation, five years later, providing the flexibility to enter new lines of business and increase profitability.

The current Broadway Bank & Trust Company office at 100 Hamilton Plaza.

In anticipating the future, Kolben sees Broadway Bank as being in a favorable position with regard to interstate banking and other competitive factors. "People still want to do business with a local, community bank where they know everyone," he says. "Customers want to feel like they are individually important to their bank, not just one of the crowd."

Broadway Bank & Trust Company looks eagerly to a future of increased competition. "We must be an efficient, market-driven operation," says Sukenick. "And we must remain innovative, such as by developing a merchant banking operation to assist entrepreneurs in the selling and purchasing of small and medium-size businesses."

ST. JOSEPH'S HOSPITAL AND MEDICAL CENTER

It was in 1867 that a small group of nuns, all Sisters of Charity of St. Elizabeth, first organized what was to become St. Joseph's Hospital and Medical Center.

That first hospital was a small wooden house with 12 beds in downtown Paterson. Today St. Joseph's is a multidivisional medical center with an acute care hospital in Paterson, a nursing home in Montclair, the innovative Clifton Family Practice Associates in Clifton, and St. Joseph's Family Health Center near St. Joseph's original home in downtown Paterson.

Now in its second century of service and still operated by the Sisters of Charity, St. Joseph's Hospital and Medical Center has become one of the leading health care institutions in New Jersey. From its original dozen beds it has grown into one of the state's largest medical centers, offering 701 beds, 50 bassinets, and a broad range of diagnostic and therapeutic services. The current major expansion and renovation program, begun in 1985, will add more than 50 new beds and enhanced care facilities to the main hospital complex.

More than 200,000 patients of every race and creed turn to St. Joseph's each year for care. They come from throughout New Jersey to be treated by the institution's staff of more than 550 physicians with 24,000 of them as inpatients. More than 38,000 are treated at the Emergency Room, and some 115,000 outpatient visits are recorded annually by the specialized ambulatory care units. This modern medical care complex of operating units and services has its foundations deep in the history of the Silk City.

Two years after the end of the Civil War Paterson's economy was thriving. Thousands of immigrants from many lands flocked to the tiny city to work in the locomotive plants, shops, and textile and silk mills. While some attained great wealth and comfort, multitudes suffered from illness, industrial injury, disease, and the ravages of neglect. Sanitary measures were grossly inadequate, and raging epidemics were frequent events. There

In 1910 horse-drawn ambulances carried patients to St. Joseph's Hospital in times of emergency.

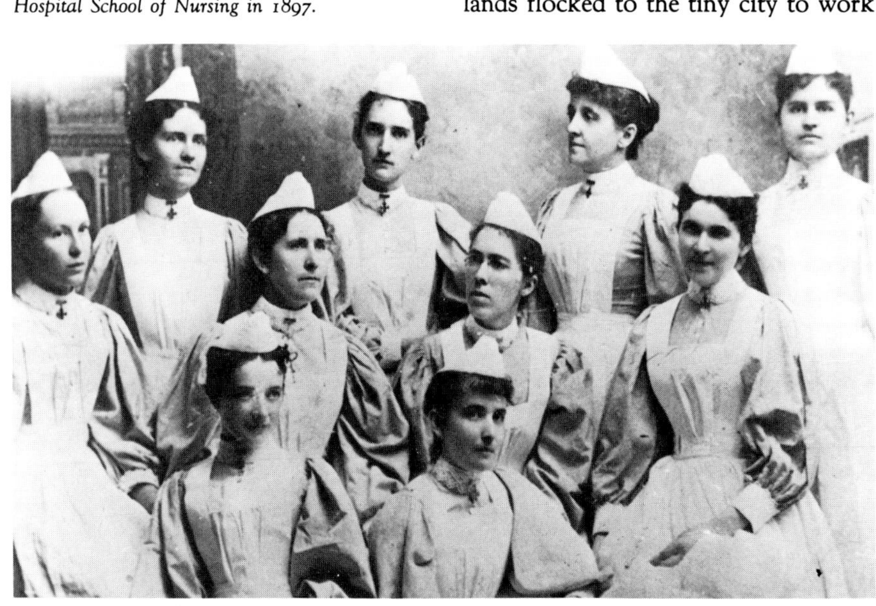

The first graduating class of nurses from St. Joseph's Hospital School of Nursing in 1897.

The Fonda Estate House, circa 1880, site of the present St. Joseph's Hospital and Medical Center.

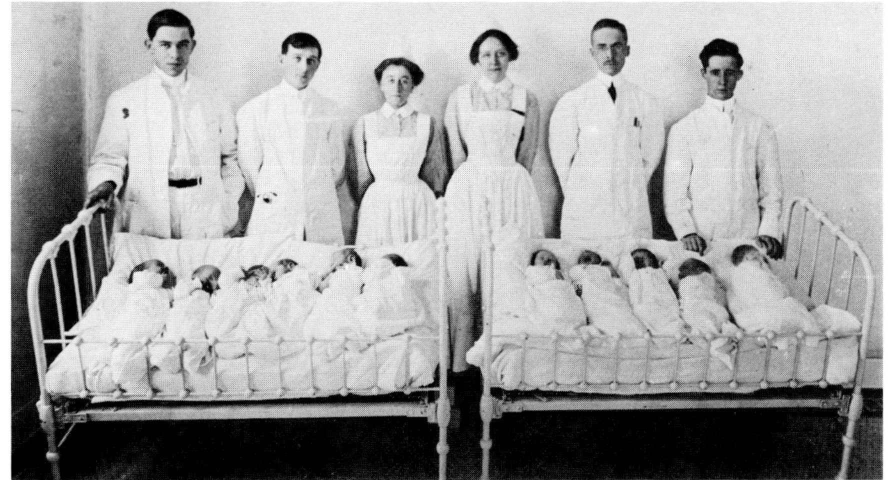

Then as now babies have always been St. Joseph's Hospital's business.

was no place for the sick and poor to be treated.

That situation began to change in 1867, when five Sisters of Charity came to Paterson to minister to the needs of laborers and their families when they were ill or injured. Beginning in their small frame house on Market Street, within a year the Sisters had purchased the Fonda house and farm on Main Street where St. Joseph's still stands. Capacity there stood at 32 free beds.

The little hospital struggled, spurred on by the faith and dedication of the Sisters. They scrubbed, cooked, tended sheep and pigs, and grew fruit and vegetables—all while pursuing their primary mission, nursing the sick. They were never out of debt, often taking in laundry and begging pennies at the factory gates to purchase food and medicine for those who sought their help. No one was ever turnèd away.

Those early Sisters and physicians were pioneers not only in building an institution to serve the people of the city, but also in developing innovative practices that have become standard operations in hospitals to this day. In 1870 they established the first outpatient dispensary, and 14 years later they opened the first isolation ward for victims of the terrible epidemics that swept through the city.

Surgery was first introduced at St. Joseph's in 1882, and by the end of the decade surgeons were performing nearly 300 operations per year. The first pathology laboratory began operations in 1887, and the School of Nursing was opened seven years later. Fourteen babies were born at the hospital in 1895—the year the Sisters opened the maternity ward.

From those roots the modern St. Joseph's Hospital and Medical Center sprung forth throughout the twentieth century. Each successive year or building program brought about dramatic changes in the hospital's patient capacity and in the services it offered. Whether it be the scientific breakthroughs of the X-ray and the opening of the radiology department in 1902 or its expansion to 250 beds in 1912, St. Joseph's has built on a tradition of dedication and service to humankind.

St. Joseph's Hospital and Medical Center continues to grow nearly 120 years after its founding—not only in bricks and mortar, but, more importantly, in excellence and in the scope of its services. While the institution's physical plant has changed markedly from that first 12-bed wooden house, the Sisters of Charity remain committed to their original objectives. The whispering rustle of the Sisters' floor-length habits is heard in the corridors of the hospital no more, as the Sisters opt for more conventional lay attire. But they have never wavered in their commitment to provide the best possible care, particularly to the sick poor.

Under the direction of its president, Sister Jane Frances Brady, S.C., St. Joseph's Hospital and Medical Center looks forward to the completion of the current building program, which will provide larger and better facilities for patients and staff and provide the tools for twenty-first-century medicine.

The institution has marshalled its resources in such key areas as primary care through the Clifton Family Practice Associates and its Family Health Center in Paterson, highly comprehensive cardiac diagnostic and surgical units, crucial perinatal care for high-risk infants and mothers, renal dialysis that literally keeps hundreds alive each day, emergency care, and St. Vincent's Nursing Home, which provides long-term care and such services as day care for families caring for elderly members.

St. Joseph's Hospital and Medical Center may be more than a century old, but its vigor and commitment are undiminished.

The model for St. Joseph's (new) Hospital and Medical Center due for completion in 1989.

BROGAN CADILLAC-OLDSMOBILE

The post-World War I boom was at its zenith when Tom Brogan, an exceptional car salesman, started his Cadillac-LaSalle dealership in Paterson. Brogan, only 29 years old when he opened his showroom on Market Street, was a nationally recognized sales leader in the industry. He began his career with the E.A. Browne Cadillac dealership and quickly rose through the sales ranks to become Browne's partner before purchasing the company outright in 1927.

The Cadillac automobile even then

Thomas J. Brogan, founder and chairman of Brogan Cadillac-Oldsmobile Company.

was recognized as the premiere American car. And the Brogan dealership developed a reputation for personal service and competitive pricing, leading to early success for the company.

Despite Brogan's business acumen, outside forces bore down on the industry and nation. The Stock Market Crash of 1929 precipitated the Great Depression. This economic calamity destroyed many businesses—including auto dealerships—in its wake.

The crisis proved to be the acid test of Brogan's business and management abilities. Under his resolute leadership,

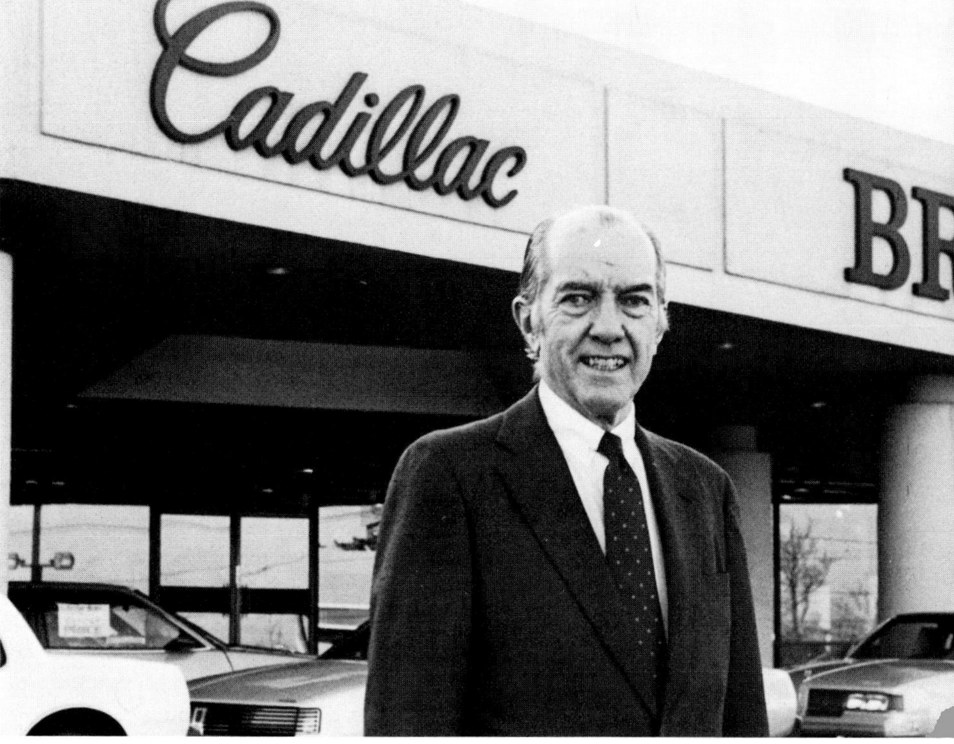

Thomas J. Brogan, Jr., president of Brogan Cadillac-Oldsmobile, at his modern dealership on Route 46 in Totowa.

Brogan Cadillac weathered the storm. This was made possible by Brogan's wise choice of vehicles, as the Cadillac continued to be favored by a select market even in the depths of the Depression. The dealership's sales volume was reduced, but Brogan continued operations throughout the 1930s. The LaSalle line was dropped, but in 1932 Brogan added the moderately priced Oldsmobile line.

During the early years Brogan Cadillac-Oldsmobile was located at Madison Avenue opposite 16th Avenue. (The distinctive Cadillac crest is still visible on the building's walls.) It was moved in 1938 to the 505 Ellison Street site it would occupy for more than 40 years.

In addition to the new car showroom on Ellison Street, the dealership had a used car department at 1065 Market Street. Despite the Depression Brogan Cadillac-Oldsmobile served a wide market, from the superior Cadillac to the medium-price Oldsmobile as well as a full selection of previously owned cars.

Surviving the Depression years through the determination of Tom Brogan, the dealership looked to the 1940s as a period of growth and prosperity. World War II proved to be the greatest test in Brogan Cadillac-Oldsmobile's existence.

While the Depression had severely limited the automobile market, the war, for all practical purposes, destroyed it. For a period of nearly five years virtually no new cars were produced by American plants. Actually there were no automobile plants, as they had been pressed into service assembling trucks, tanks, and other implements of war. The Brogan Cadillac-Oldsmobile dealership faced no greater challenge. With no cars to sell and his staff going to war, Brogan again rose to meet the crisis.

The dealership's showroom on Ellison Street was leased to Wright Aeronautical Corporation as a school

Following World War II Brogan Cadillac-Oldsmobile resumed its position as Paterson's leading automobile showroom and dealership at its Ellison Street location.

for Allied engineers. Business operations were shifted to the used car department on Market Street. There Brogan and his limited staff dedicated themselves to keeping older cars on the road through top mechanical service—and the sale of whatever vehicles came along.

With the war's end Brogan's son, Thomas Jr., joined the company after a stint in the Army Air Corps. By 1946 the first postwar vehicles began to roll off the assembly lines, and the dealership reopened its Ellison Street showroom with a gala celebration.

The 1940s and 1950s were highlighted by Brogan Cadillac-Oldsmobile's broad expansion. Thomas Sr. became a distributor and opened branches in Ridgewood (run by his son, J. Peter) and Passaic (under nephew Thomas J. Ely). New facilities were constructed in Ridgewood in 1948, and the Passaic operation moved to Clifton two years later with a new showroom at the strategic intersection of Main Avenue and Route 3.

While the business expanded, Thomas Jr. spent two years attending the General Motors Institute. Following that training, he entered an apprenticeship with his father in which he learned operations from the ground up.

The apple doesn't fall far from the tree, and Tom Jr. also specialized in sales. Today Thomas Sr. serves as chairman of Brogan Cadillac-Oldsmobile, while his son is president and oversees daily operations.

The senior Brogan's interests ranged beyond the immediate needs of his business as the company continued to expand during the 1960s and 1970s. A civic leader, he served as Paterson Police Commissioner and chairman of the North Jersey Water Supply Commission. He also was a trustee of St. Joseph's Hospital and Medical Center in Paterson and Valley Hospital in Ridgewood, and serves as director of the First Fidelity Bank.

His interest in horse power—the four-legged variety—led to his service for more than 20 years on the New Jersey State Racing Commission, 16 of which were as chairman. He also served as president of the National Association of State Racing Commissioners.

After more than 40 years at the three-acre Ellison Street location, the dealership had outgrown its headquarters. This was rectified by relocation in 1982 to a six-acre site with an ultramodern showroom at the intersection of Route 46 East and Union Avenue in Totowa, part of the greater Paterson area the company has served for 60 years.

With three major locations in the prime Passaic and Bergen counties market by the early 1980s, Brogan Cadillac-Oldsmobile's expansion was not at an end. The company looked to new horizons by purchasing a Cadillac dealership located in North Brunswick within the growing mid-Jersey market.

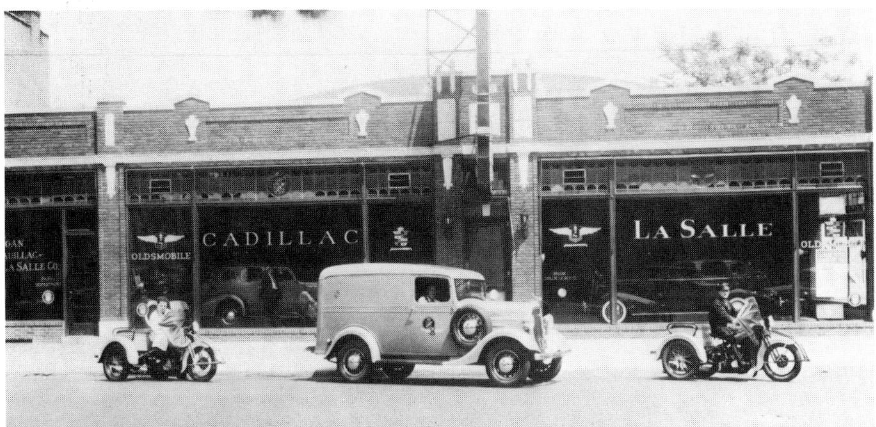

The Brogan Cadillac-LaSalle Company was located on Madison Avenue during the 1930s.

FIRST FIDELITY BANK, N.A.-NORTH JERSEY

The people and business community of Paterson and Passaic County are served by many first-quality commercial banks. The oldest in continuous service is First Fidelity Bank, N.A.-North Jersey, whose earliest predecessor, The First National Bank, was founded nearly 125 years ago.

The year was 1864. Bloody civil war pitted one section of the nation against another. Great battles brought armies together in such places as Manassas, Antietam, Vicksburg, and Gettysburg. The slaughter was monstrous in scale; the American Civil War was truly the first "total war."

A portrait of John J. Brown, the first president of The First National Bank of Paterson.

While the outcome was still in doubt, the trend as 1864 opened was finally beginning to turn in favor of the Union, led by President Abraham Lincoln and soon to come under the military command of General Ulysses S. Grant. A major factor serving to benefit the military fortunes of the Union forces was the enormous industrial capacity of the North. Paterson, New Jersey, where American industrialization had taken its first, unsteady steps, experienced a booming economy based on the war's insatiable appetite for locomotives and textiles, as well as for the implements of war.

In the midst of this great financial upsurge, the inadequacies of local banking services became apparent to industrial and business leaders based in Paterson. Those influential men began forming the city's first federally chartered bank on January 29, 1864, under the initiative of George M. Stimson, who subscribed for more than 90 percent of the new institution's stock. Due to Stimson's subsequent illness and the lack of will on the part of the organizers, the new bank still had not opened to the public by July of that year, and its directors voted to liquidate.

Then John Jackson Brown stepped

The First National Bank of Paterson, the original predecessor of today's First Fidelity Bank, began business at this location in 1864.

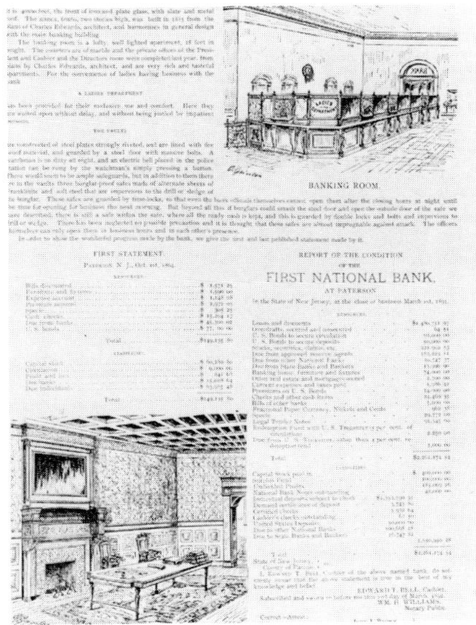
BANKING ROOM.

FIRST STATEMENT.

REPORT OF THE CONDITION OF THE FIRST NATIONAL BANK, AT PATERSON

Here a reproduction of a page describes the Directors' Room and the Banking Room of the First National Bank headquarters at 125 Ellison Street during the 1890s.

into the picture. Brown, who was elected Paterson's first mayor in 1854 after its incorporation as a city, had come to Paterson in 1822 at the age of five. Drugstore clerk, furrier, and dry goods dealer in turn, Brown was a successful merchant and a dedicated civic leader.

Despite considerable obstacles, Brown raised the $100,000 to capitalize the revived First National Bank. Serving with him on the first functioning board of directors were such captains of Paterson's industry and commerce as John Cooke, John Reynolds, Henry B. Crosby, John N. Terhune, Henry M. Low, Jonathan S. Christie, Josiah P. Huntoon, John Swinburne, Patrick Curran, Edward C. May, William Gledhill, and George M. Stimson.

First National Bank's first building (at 125 Ellison Street) was destroyed in the Great Fire of 1902 in Paterson.

Brown's colleagues elected him president of the institution on September 17, 1864—the same day 21-year-old Edward T. Bell was appointed to the equally vital cashier's position. Bell, although young, had more than four years experience in banking. Between them, the two men guided The First National Bank through its initial 50 years of existence.

The institution formally opened for business on September 21, 1864. Its earliest offices occupied the parlors of a three-story brick building on the west side of Main Street (then No. 192, now No. 240), where Colonel C.G. Garrison had lived for many years. The parlors had been "fitted up for business, with little expense," an early bank report declared.

The First National Bank grew, and on January 1, 1865, capital was increased from $100,000 to $250,000. Deposits had climbed to $256,000. By February 1866 the institution occupied street floor space in the Congress Hall Hotel at 235 Main Street.

Again rented quarters proved inadequate. By January 1869 a committee of the board of directors recommended the construction of a permanent home for the bank. Two months later a site was chosen at the corner of Washington and Ellison streets, and on February 21, 1870, ground was broken. The cornerstone was laid less than six months later, on August 9.

A major event in the early history of what would become First Fidelity Bank, N.A.-North Jersey, took place on April 27, 1871. The First National Bank of Paterson moved into its grand new four-story, iron-construction building, erected at a cost of $126,000. At that time the institution had a surplus of $125,000 in addition to its capital of $400,000, deposits of

The Second National Bank building (now First Fidelity Bank's Market Street office) was one of the few fireproof buildings that survived the Great Fire of 1902. The burned-out shell of the City Hall is at the left.

$838,000, and circulating notes worth $315,000.

The new bank building became a center for the bustling city's business community, with the post office and Western Union Telegraph renting space there. In addition, several attorneys leased rooms on the top floors. First National reserved only the second floor for itself.

Under the able leadership of Brown and Bell the bank thrived despite setbacks from a series of financial panics in 1873, 1884, and 1896. When Bell retired as president in 1921 (having succeeded Brown in 1894), First National had successfully weathered five major business recessions, three wars, devastating fires and floods, and tumultuous labor strikes.

Perhaps most indicative of the bank's institutional fiber was how it handled the effects of the disastrous Great Fire of February 1902, which razed much of Paterson's downtown business district—including The First National Bank's building. Under Bell's direction, the institution established temporary quarters at Main and Market streets and then purchased a small building on Church Street to use while a new building was being constructed. Meanwhile the bank endeavored to assist the city itself in its rebuilding efforts by facilitating loans or advances in every possible way.

Over the years The First National Bank of Paterson formed the taproot of what has become a family tree of banking facilities serving all of Passaic County and into Bergen, Hudson, Middlesex, and Morris counties.

Beginning in 1946 with its purchase of Paterson National Bank (established in 1889), The First National Bank began a series of acquisitions of local banks to form a broad-based financial institution offering the most modern of banking services. Those consolidations included the Second National Bank (founded in 1865) and acquired in 1948; The Linares and Rescigno Bank (1920), absorbed in 1956; and the United States Trust Co. of Paterson (1903), consolidated in 1951.

First Fidelity's modern headquarters on Union Boulevard in Totowa is the hub of the bank's operations throughout North Jersey.

Outside Paterson the expansion brought in the North Jersey National Bank of Pompton Lakes, whose roots went back to 1915 before being absorbed in 1953. The First National Bank of Bloomingdale (1925) was purchased in 1955, joining both the First National Bank of Clifton (1921) and Clifton Trust Co. (1915), which were absorbed in 1949.

In 1959 the institution's name was changed to First National Bank of Passaic County, reflecting its 17 banking locations around the county. With its further expansion outside the county during the late 1960s and early 1970s, it became The First National Bank of New Jersey.

Beginning in September 1983 the old First National Bank of Paterson made its most dramatic structural change when it joined First National State Bancorporation, linking a tradition of service and growth in Passaic County with New Jersey's largest bank holding company, with origins that date back to 1812. Operating since November 1, 1984, under the name First Fidelity Bank, N.A.-North Jersey, reflecting the broad horizons of financial services to local communities, businesses, and individuals, the institution that had its origins in Colonel Garrison's parlors is setting the pace of modern service in the space age.

First Fidelity Bank, N.A.-North Jersey, continues to provide innovative services—from the state's first Customer Service Department to conveniently located "supermarket branches," trend-setting computerization of services, and PACE, the bill paying by telephone system. Today First Fidelity Bank employs more than 1,000 people in its Administrative Center in Totowa, a newly opened auxiliary center in Clifton, and 39 branches, in addition to 20 automatic teller machines that provide 24-hour banking convenience.

First Fidelity Bank, N.A.-North Jersey, has evolved since its founding as a depository geared to meet the modest needs of business and industry in a small industrial city. Now it is a full-service, modern financial institution dedicated to consumers and commercial customers throughout northern New Jersey in an ever-changing financial environment, serving them at home, throughout the state and nation, and around the world.

John Jackson Brown and Edward T. Bell would be proud.

HUNZIKER, MERREY & JONES, P.A.

Gustav A. Hunziker and Edward F. Merrey belonged to a small fraternity of influential attorneys who practiced their profession in Paterson from the end of the nineteenth century into the middle of the twentieth century.

These two men never practiced together. At crucial times they represented opposing litigants, and staunchly supported different political parties. Their separate law firms, a generation later, found a mutuality of interest that led to the formation of Hunziker, Merrey & Jones, P.A.

In earlier days business was often conducted on the sidewalk during casual meetings throughout the day. Both Hunziker and Merrey, the latter almost until the time of his death in 1974, were often seen in Paterson. Well liked and widely recognized, both were known as men of character and integrity and as influential leaders in the city.

Edward F. Merrey had begun his practice in 1895 after attending what is now New York University Law School and reading law. He became city counsel in 1907 and was involved with the statute that first established a strong mayor form of government that controlled Paterson for the next 60 years. He also was involved with litigation against Public Service, the water company, and the Erie Railroad, all on behalf of the city. He served the city in various capacities for more than 30 years.

During their time Edward F. Merrey (left) and Gustav A. Hunziker (right) practiced in separate law firms, but today their names belong to the modern firm of Hunziker, Merrey & Jones, P.A.

Gustav A. Hunziker had emigrated as an infant from Basel, Switzerland, and followed his father into employment in Paterson's silk mills after completing the seventh grade in school. After taking the postal examination, however, he was encouraged to study law, and was admitted to the bar in 1899. Perhaps because of his childhood employment in the mills, Hunziker represented some of the workers during the Great Strike of 1913, when they were tried for unlawful assembly. He later became a member of the State Board of Education and served as its president for 15 years prior to his death in 1951.

The professional staff of Hunziker, Merrey & Jones includes (left to right) Steven J. Carras, Susan E. Champion, Edward F. Merrey, Jr., Walter J. Hunziker, Walter J. Hunziker, Jr., and Robert A. Jones.

The two law offices, each headed by the only son of its founder, merged in 1982, and now occupy a suite of offices in the historic First National Bank Building behind city hall on Ellison Street. The firm has maintained an office in the center of West Milford since 1958, one of the first law firms to be located in that up-county township.

Hunziker, Merrey & Jones is today comprised of six attorneys. Walter J. Hunziker, Jr., Robert A. Jones, Susan E. Champion, and Steven J. Carras join with Walter J. Hunziker, and Edward F. Merrey, Jr., in the office.

The firm has a general practice ranging from corporation and business law, through real estate and land planning, to wills and estate administration. The broad focus of the firm is principally related to individuals and their property and problems.

Although Hunziker, Merrey & Jones, P.A., is a relatively small firm in today's world, its influence and roots in Paterson and Passaic County extend back through generations. Its members continue to devote their time, skills, and professional abilities to the service of their clients, local communities, and institutions.

BRITT BROKERAGE COMPANY, INC.

Adiel Brito Sutter studied architecture in Peru. Today he is the architect of growing businesses, anchored by Britt Brokerage Company, Inc., in a land he has called home for only 17 years. The progression from immigrant to entrepreneur is a story filled with confidence in one's abilities, determination, quality performance, and a dream for the future.

"Lucho" Brito is such an individual. Born into an enterprising family that owned a seafood import/export business, he overcame reverses that forced him to leave his studies after only a year. Then, after a rebuilding effort that revived the business and brought him into this country in search of equipment for expansion, he found himself struck down again—this time by a military dictatorship that seized his business.

No latter-day Job lamenting his fate, Brito set out with the limited funds at his disposal to make a new life for his family and himself. And that new life began in Paterson.

Living off what money he had saved, Brito sought to apply his interest in cars to earning his way in his new country. Beginning as an unskilled laborer in a Clifton auto body shop, he was able to open his own body shop in Paterson within five years. Working alone, often from dawn to the early hours of the following morning, Brito struggled to make a go of the business he started in 1977.

Noted for quality service on such makes as BMW, Mercedes Benz, and Porsche, he expanded the business to include wholesale distribution of used vehicles. As his work so closely involved dealing with insurance companies, Brito decided to study and open his own insurance brokerage. That organization, Britt Brokerage Company, Inc., has become the cornerstone of Brito's diverse activities.

He built his business by representing such major insurance firms as The Travellers to a primarily Latino market—small businesses such as restaurants, liquor stores, retail shops—with whom Brito had a special "simpatico."

Today Britt Brokerage Company has two offices each in Paterson and Passaic, with a new facility being launched in Union City. The firm specializes in commercial insurance for a broad spectrum of businesses. In addition to commercial insurance services, the company also provides broad automobile and other insurance programs.

The student architect of 25 years ago is today a master builder of businesses in addition to the insurance brokerage firm, including the auto body shop, a liquor store, and travel agency in Paterson, as well as a radiator and air-conditioner service center in Brooklyn. And the enterprising spirit extends into the Brito family. His wife is the owner of a successful clothing and gift shop in Paterson.

Adiel Brito Sutter looks to the future for his sons, 20 and 15 years old, respectively. He is trying to teach them the responsibilities of proper stewardship of these enterprises, which provide employment for nearly 30 people.

He often works seven days a week. But to Lucho Brito, the effort and fatigue are worth the opportunity to grow unhindered in a free society.

Adiel Brito Sutter and his wife, Graciela, are the owners of Britt Brokerage Company, Inc.

JERSEY LIFT TRUCK COMPANY

One of the exciting facets of the American economic system is how men and women recognize opportunity and then marshal the initiative and discipline to pursue it. The lines of business that people enter and transform into successful careers are like penny candy selections made by children years ago. America's economic "candy store" holds hundreds of such possibilities for success—and they are not limited to any elite group. Opportunity, in so many ways, is open to all.

Edwin Gerena, owner and president of Jersey Lift Truck Company, is a prime example of a person's willingness to commit himself to the task of building a business. Nearly 30 years later he is still looking forward and creating new approaches and new opportunities.

Brooklyn, New York, was Gerena's home. After four years' service in the Army during the early 1950s, he worked for a forklift company as a mechanic. But Gerena, even then, was a restless man who wanted to be his own boss.

In 1956 he started Ed's Forklift Service in Brooklyn. He visited companies and worked on their forklift equipment from his own truck. The following year Gerena was looking westward, as so many industrious pioneers had done before. He and a partner, Jerry Siano, purchased Jersey Lift Truck Company, which was located in Paterson's Bunker Hill section on Bleeker Street.

For the first months Gerena and Siano did the reverse commute from Brooklyn to their business housed in a converted two-car garage. As in Brooklyn, they traveled to their customers' places of business and serviced forklift equipment on premises. They worked for local dye houses, warehouses, manufacturers, and trucking firms in Paterson, Clifton, Passaic, and into southern Bergen County.

The business grew slowly. In 1962 Gerena and Siano purchased the 42 Alabama Avenue site. The building was small, only 2,500 square feet, but it served their needs. In 1967 Gerena bought out his partner's share in the business. A few years later he increased the size of the building to 7,500 square feet and added additional property on Alabama Avenue.

Today Jersey Lift Truck Company continues to serve its core area, providing full service, including rentals, sales of reconditioned equipment, and repairs. But Gerena is looking for new horizons.

He and his son, Edwin Jr., are developing an ambitious short-term forklift equipment rental business dedicated to providing top-notch forklift units on an hourly, daily, or monthly basis. They have a new division called Rentalift. Their second rental location is operating in East Brunswick, near the Route 1 corridor.

"Efficiency, along with a desire to be independent, has always been my goal," says Edwin Gerena, Sr. "We have automated many of our backroom operations, and my son is applying new business and marketing techniques to the company. We feel that the rental business, in which we service the equipment that we rent out, is the best direction for the company to take over the long term."

With entrepreneurs like Edwin Gerena, Paterson and Passaic County will continue to be major focal points of economic activity in the future as they have been in years gone by.

Edwin Gerena founded his first business, Ed's Forklift Service, in Brooklyn in 1956 to service factory forklifts from his own truck. With the purchase of the Jersey Lift Truck Company and a move to Paterson, Gerena established the present sales, rental, and repair business.

DE JONG IRON WORKS, INC.

Throughout its history Paterson has been a community of enterprising men and women from many backgrounds who seize the initiative and persevere in building their own businesses. To these individuals, owning and nurturing a business is a high calling that is to be carried down through the generations.

The De Jong Iron Works, located at 223-231 Godwin Avenue, epitomizes the concept of a "family business" that has adapted and grown from generation to generation. Founded in Paterson by Minerd De Jong in 1908 and incorporated six years later, the firm has witnessed the arrival of the fourth generation of the De Jong family in the operation of the business.

Minerd De Jong was an enterprising carpenter who also sold iron fencing—a symbol of prosperity early in this century—and other steel products. That sideline became highly successful, and De Jong decided to operate his own plant. Originally located at 49 Pearl Street, De Jong Iron Works produced primarily fences, ornamental metalwork, and other miscellaneous iron products for home use. The business quickly grew and was relocated to larger quarters at 187-189 Lafayette Street in 1913.

In the 10 years that followed De Jong Iron Works further diversified its product line to include fire escapes, metal cellar doors for businesses as well as homes, and, ultimately, custom structural steel for the construction of industrial plants, office buildings, and other edifices. By the 1920s space was again at a premium, and in 1922 the firm erected a modern facility at its present site on Godwin Avenue in Paterson.

The boom years of the 1920s ended with the Great Depression, but Minerd De Jong, along with his brothers, Charles, Jacob, and Fred, broadened the company's products in order to increase its market base. A major new product line, which continues to be important to this day, was the fabrication of concrete-filled support columns for industrial, commercial, and residential construction.

Maynard (left) and Ed De Jong are the third generation of the De Jong family to operate De Jong Iron Works.

During World War II De Jong Ironworks participated in the victory effort by furnishing specially fabricated steel products for defense-related needs. At that time Aaron De Jong, Minerd's son, joined the company; he later became its general manager.

With the end of the war came two important events for the company: Current president Martin De Jong, Fred De Jong's son, joined his cousin, Aaron, in the business, and there was a construction boom as new GI housing was erected throughout North Jersey. De Jong Iron Works provided the vital steel central beams, railings, cellar doors, and other appurtenances for the new homes.

The expanding office, commercial, and warehousing development in the northern part of the state—and throughout the country—led to the company's increasingly active role in fabricating structural steel that began in the 1960s. Today such giants of industry as Sandvik Steel, Exxon, and Hoffmann-La Roche rank among the end-users of De Jong structural steel products. Truly this Paterson company has seen its products used throughout the nation.

Now Aaron's son, Maynard, and nephew, Edward, have assumed active management of De Jong Iron Works, Inc. Aaron's grandson, David, recently joined the company as a representative of the fourth generation of the De Jong family to carry on the business.

De Jong Iron Works looks today much the same as it did in this photo from the 1940s.

COLE, GEANEY, YAMNER & BYRNE, P.A.

Paterson was always a lawyer's town. As the county seat, and as the leading commercial and industrial locus from the nineteenth through the twentieth centuries, the city was—as it is today—a magnet drawing phalanxes of attorneys to its core.

The law firm of Cole, Geaney, Yamner & Byrne, P.A., although of more recent vintage, ranks with those of an earlier age for service to businesses and individuals, not only in Paterson and its environs but also throughout the Northeast. This firm, which has a broad, general practice ranging from banking, real estate, and commercial law to taxation, estates, and litigation in all state and federal trial and appellate courts, was begun through the merger of the practices of Murray L. Cole and John F. Geaney, Jr., in 1967.

Cole had been a partner with Daniel Parke Lieblich, who left the firm to pursue a corporate career. Geaney had been a partner with his well-known father-in-law, Hugh C. Spernow, who was appointed to the bench. Shortly thereafter, Morris Yamner, who had been an associate of Cole's and a former deputy attorney general, became the third partner, and a few years later John J. Byrne III became the fourth name partner.

The firm now includes 11 partners and an equal number of associates with William F. Hinchliffe and retired Superior Court Judge Irving I. Rubin of counsel. The practice is headquartered in offices occupying portions of two floors of the Broadway Bank building at 100 Hamilton Plaza, which dominates Paterson's bustling downtown business district.

While the firm serves a diverse and demanding clientele, its members—from senior partners to most recent associates—make time to take leadership roles in professional and civic endeavors.

For example, Murray L. Cole is a trustee of the New Jersey State Bar Association, presides as chairman of the board of Montclair State College, sits as a director of United Jersey Bank, and also serves as a member of the National Advisory Board for the Boy Scouts of America.

John F. Geaney, Jr., is the current president of the Passaic County Bar Association and is a trustee of Don Bosco College, the St. Joseph's Home for the Elderly, and the Family Counseling Service of Passaic County. Morris Yamner serves as a director of the Broadway Bank and is a member of the board of directors of the Daughters of Miriam, Passaic-Clifton YM-YWHA, and the Jewish Federation of Clifton-Passaic. Geaney, Byrne, and Michael Mopsick, another firm partner, all recently served as chairman of the Passaic County Ethics Commmittee—appointed by the New Jersey Supreme Court.

As Paterson and its surrounding communities were served in the past by able and dedicated, public-minded attorneys, that tradition is being continued today by reputable firms such as Cole, Geaney, Yamner & Byrne, P.A., in serving the needs of individuals, organizations, businesses, and communities.

The late Judge Hugh C. Spernow.

The other partners of Cole, Geaney, Yamner & Byrne are (standing, left to right) Peter R. Bray and William D. Green, and (seated, left to right) George W. Parsons, Vincent A. Siano, and Gary S. Redish. Not pictured: Michael D. Mopsick and Steven Brawer.

The four partners for whom the firm is named are (seated, left to right) John F. Geaney, Jr., and Murray L. Cole, and (standing, left to right) John J. Bryne III and Morris Yamner.

TWINBROOK TRUCK MAINTENANCE, INC.

Entrepreneurial spirit is not solely in the domain of the past. The genius of Ford, Carnegie, and others who built business structures within this country can be found today in the towns and cities of Passaic County and the surrounding region. Carl Dorsey, founder and president of Twinbrook Truck Maintenance, Inc., is a vital example of the continuing drive and creativity of the modern entrepreneur.

Dorsey, even as a child, tinkered with anything mechanical, so it was natural that he should be working with the trucks and heavy equipment of the Samuel Braen Contracting Company. Now, more than 30 years later, Dorsey heads the largest new truck sales and service dealership in Paterson. In addition to the dealership featuring Mercedes, Isuzu, and Mitsubishi Fuso trucks, Dorsey's allied operations include truck fabrication, body work and painting, and towing and road services.

The road to success took many twists and turns, leavened with hard work. But Carl Dorsey's own natural mechanical talents have always been at the fore. While serving in the Army in the 1950s, Dorsey was one of a select group of technicians assigned to work with guided missile pioneer Wernher Von Braun in this country's first efforts reaching into outer space. Following military service, he attended the Cummins Engine School and returned to the Samuel Braen Contracting Company as an expert mechanic in diesel engines and drive trains. Then, in 1964, Dorsey began a quest to build his own business.

That first venture, the genesis for his continuing enterprises today, was a truck service operation begun in 1964. Working nights and weekends in a rented garage in Franklin Lakes while holding down a full-time position, Dorsey's Twinbrook Truck Maintenance proved successful. The following year he established a trucking firm with two other partners, in which he was responsible for the vehicles' maintenance, while still operating Twinbrook and working for the Samuel Braen Contracting Company.

By 1966 Dorsey was devoting himself full time to his growing business interests and moved Twinbrook to 278 Greenwood Avenue in Midland Park. Within the next year he purchased his partners' interests in the trucking firm.

After selling off the trucking operation in 1969, Dorsey focused his energies on servicing trucks and heavy equipment of all makes and models. The business grew quickly, and a second location, on Goffle Road in Hawthorne, was added the following year.

Dorsey's peripatetic nature brought him to take over the former Reinauer truck repair facility on Route 17 in 1972, which he operated for the next five years while continuing the truck servicing business in Hawthorne.

The year 1977 brought a real

The general offices of Twinbrook Truck Maintenance at 752-758 20th Avenue.

change in direction for Dorsey's enterprising spirit that would have a major impact on his business fortunes. The Route 17 truck stop was more than 90-percent transient in nature. Trucks came in and went out 24 hours a day, six days a week. But Dorsey wanted to know his customers, so he targeted those companies that operated their own trucks and required high-quality, reliable service. The transient trade just didn't fit in.

With the divestiture of the Route 17 site, Dorsey centered his attention on the Hawthorne service location. As the business grew it attracted favorable attention, and the Mercedes Benz Truck Division approached Dorsey to start up a dealership. By the end of 1977 Twinbrook's sales, service, and parts business grossed $1.5 million.

The growth of the firm's sales and service volume by the early 1980s provided the impetus for Dorsey to seek larger facilities. After investigating many sites throughout the Passaic County area, Paterson's strategic location near major highways, coupled with its large regional market base, made the city the prime candidate for the Twinbrook Truck Maintenance headquarters.

And the city responded. Mayor Frank Graves enthusiastically supported Dorsey's plan to become the first new truck dealer in Paterson in years. In September 1983 Twinbrook Truck Maintenance located its new headquarters at 752-758 20th Avenue just off Route 20 and easily accessible to routes 4, 46, and I-80.

Within three months business had more than doubled, but the entrepreneurial drive in Carl Dorsey could not be stilled. He added truck fabricating and alterations—providing customers with specialized features for their own requirements—which has become a major part of the company's overall business. He then formed Greenwood Vehicle Service on East 26th Street, where customized painting and signage, as well as body repairs, are provided for numerous local businesses.

Closed out of domestic makes of lighter vehicles to balance the heavier Mercedes Benz trucks, Twinbrook added the Isuzu and Mitsubishi Fuso lines in order to serve a broader-based clientele. By the end of 1985 sales totaled more than five million dollars.

A branch location of Twinbrook Truck Maintenance at 107 East 27th Street.

Never standing still, Dorsey established Automotive and Commercial Services, a truck towing business run by his son, Kurt. Now Twinbrook Truck Maintenance, Inc., together with its affiliated corporations, provides broad-base truck sales and service capabilities.

Twinbrook is a balanced organization with more than 30 employees. Dorsey has structured the firm to be able to function effectively as both a service and sales organization, providing the stability to withstand the vicissitudes of business cycles.

The drive and determination of Carl Dorsey has been translated into an extremely effective, reputable business operation, one that has been joined by his wife, Carole, as head bookkeeper and daughter, Sandy, as office manager, in addition to his son, Kurt, who operates the truck towing and road service. Following Dorsey's basic credo, "I plan it and I make it happen," Twinbrook Truck Maintenance, Inc., will continue to grow as a major Partner in Progress for the greater Paterson area for many years to come.

C.J. VANDERBECK AND SON, INC.

Paterson, a leading locomotive manufacturing center from the nineteenth century into the early twentieth century, was a mecca for young men with mechanical abilities. One such individual was Cornelius J. Vanderbeck, former blacksmith and boiler mechanic at the Danforth and Cooke locomotive plant, who recognized the long-term need for the maintenance and repair of stationary heating and steam-generating equipment used by apartment buildings, schools, dye houses, and factories in and around the Cradle of the American Industrial Revolution.

In 1914 Vanderbeck began repairing boilers in the garage of the family home at 126 Knickerbocker Avenue. He concentrated his efforts on repairing industrial and commercial coal-fired boilers, which led to installation and service. He was a true artisan who earned a reputation for craftsmanship.

In 1929 his son, Edmund T., joined the company that was incorporated in 1932 as C.J. Vanderbeck and Son. That same year it relocated to 278 West Railway Avenue. During the 1920s and 1930s, despite the Depression, the firm survived due in part to the conversion of coal burners to oil.

During World War II C.J. Vanderbeck and Son, Inc., was deeply involved in the defense effort, so much so that Edmund was exempted from military service. The company worked on the Picatinny Arsenal and oil refineries and construction of the legendary Liberty ships, as well as serviced the Paterson area's industrial plants to ensure the continued output of aircraft engines, uniforms, parachutes, and other vital materials.

With the death of Cornelius Vanderbeck in 1947, Edmund continued as second generation and brought the firm into the 1950s, when a major market was servicing schools that cropped up throughout the suburbs. Concern about air quality grew, and C.J. Vanderbeck and Son became a leader in providing "scrubbers" for smokestacks in the region. The company also increased its boiler-cleaning operations to improve air quality.

The industry was becoming more conscious of safety and efficiency, and advanced electronic components came on-line for installation and servicing by C.J. Vanderbeck and Son. The boilers the company installed became streamlined, requiring more sophisticated servicing.

The third generation of the family joined the firm in 1960 when Donald, Edmund's son, took on management responsibilities when his father became ill. While Donald was "learning the business," he also initiated new marketing techniques and expanded the firm's base by going into design and engineering. As public and governmental concern about air pollution grew, he enhanced the company's technologies and services beyond regulatory standards.

C.J. Vanderbeck and Son's service area has grown beyond Paterson's immediate environs with customers ranging from Boston to Maryland but the firm's roots run deep in the city. As a result, in 1981, when the company outgrew its West Railway Avenue location, it moved to a modern new facility at 240 Marshall Street.

C.J. Vanderbeck and Son maintains its forward thrust with Donald being joined by his brothers, Kevin and Paul, who are expanding the firm's engineering and marketing capabilities. And his son, Donald Jr., who handles the company's computer operations, represents the fourth generation of the family to be involved in the business.

Today the firm employs 24 people and operates 20 vehicles, compared to fewer than five employees and one truck during the 1930s. While the days of working in a garage are long gone, one part of the business remains constant: an unbroken bloodline of hands-on service and customer contact that is still the hallmark of C.J. Vanderbeck and Son, Inc.

In 1914 Cornelius Vanderbeck, a blacksmith and boiler mechanic, began repairing boilers in the garage of his family home. Concentrating on repairing industrial and commercial coal-fired boilers, Vanderbeck soon started his own company servicing and installing these boilers. Pictured here is the truck in which Vanderbeck made service calls. Photo circa 1920

A.J. SIRIS PRODUCTS CORPORATION

The historic Royle Building, which dates back to 1888, has again become a productive Paterson location since the A.J. Siris Products Corporation moved there a few years ago.

Since the late eighteenth century Paterson has attracted many differing companies, ranging from locomotive plants to the silk mills that gave the city its lasting identification as the Silk City. While Paterson has been the home of heavy industry over the years, it has also been a fertile ground for diversified, light manufacturing firms. Today the city's attraction to these companies, such as A.J. Siris Products Corporation, remains strong.

This business was founded by its namesake in Brooklyn in 1918. Originally it produced powder puffs. With the onset of the Roaring Twenties, when women began to enjoy greater social freedom and mobility, the company developed a line of cosmetic bags. These permitted convenient carrying of cosmetics and other personal items, at work or play.

Under Siris' direction the firm expanded outside the United States with manufacturing sites in Mexico, Canada, the United Kingdom, and Germany. With the advent of World War II the company ended its German operations and committed its remaining plants to war-related production.

Following the war A.J. Siris Products Corporation found itself in new quarters in the Bronx, where it continued manufacturing cosmetics bags and accessories, but also began importing quantities of foreign-produced items. By the 1970s the company's sales consisted of 10-percent domestically produced items and 90-percent imported items.

During the 1960s A.J. Siris, who died in 1982, relinquished daily management of the business to his son, Herbert. Due to Herbert's subsequent illness, effective management of the firm passed to his son-in-law Don Ryan, who effectively changed the direction of the company.

Ryan emphasized domestic manufacturing and broader marketing so that today the firm's products are found nationwide among mass merchandisers and fine department stores and boutiques. His most significant move was to relocate A.J. Siris Products Corporation from its South Bronx home.

While in Paris on business he met Harry Haines, former editor of *The Paterson News*, who suggested that Ryan contact his father, Edward Haines, then director of economic development for Passaic County. This chance encounter, coupled with the enthusiastic support of local and county governments, led to the relocation of A.J. Siris Products Corportion in 1980 to the historic John W. Royle complex at 10 Essex Street. The company has since increased its holdings by purchasing the adjacent VanVlaaderen Building.

Today A.J. Siris Products Corporation is actively producing and marketing travel kits, cosmetic accessories, shower and slumber caps, cosmetic and toiletry cases, and plastic bottles. The firm employs 200 people, most of whom reside in or near Paterson.

The success of A.J. Siris Products Corporation and other companies like it proves that Paterson still fosters growth as it enters its third century.

N.B. FAIRCLOUGH & SON, INC.

"It boils down to the survival of the fittest," says John Fairclough, Sr., whose fuel oil business has now entered a second century of service. He rises every morning on his farm in Sussex County before 5 a.m., takes a brisk swim, and is in his office in Paterson by 6:30 a.m. Fairclough's hardy lifestyle is filled with his sons and horses—he is a well-known antique horse-drawn carriage collector—and in running a fuel business that is now into the fifth generation.

N.B. Fairclough & Son, Inc., traces its roots, as do so many Paterson businesses, to the city's heyday as the Silk City. John Sr.'s great-grandfather, Napoleon Bonaparte Fairclough, had migrated from the silk mills around Macclesfield, England, to Paterson during the mid-nineteenth century. But the silk business wasn't for him, and he soon became a coal merchant, built up a sizable business, and raised a large family.

His only son, Napoleon Bonaparte Fairclough, Jr., started a rival coal business in 1882 from a pier on the Morris Canal in Paterson. His business philosophy was to sell only the best and to aim for the larger customers. The mansions of mill owners and merchants had cellars that could hold many tons of coal, and these were filled in the summer when the price was at its lowest. By getting that business, the Fairclough wagons were kept rolling throughout the year, hauling coal at about $1.35 per ton delivered. (It now sells for about $140 per ton.)

By the end of World War I Pennsylvania hard coal was being brought into Paterson by rail, and the Fairclough business was moved to its present location by the rail side at 800 East 27th Street. N.B.'s son, John, joined the business, which had two dozen wagons, each with a team of horses.

John H. Fairclough, Sr., president and owner of N.B. Fairclough & Son, Inc., of Paterson.

Napoleon B. Fairclough (1864-1948), founder.

The teamsters day began at 6 a.m., harnessing their own horses and working much past dark for one dollar, then a normal day's wage. Each teamster was given two horse blankets: one he sat on, and the other he wrapped around his legs in winter. When the coal was being unloaded, the blankets were thrown over the horses.

The horses were hard-working, intelligent animals. When the teamsters cut the day's dust from their throats with a tankard or two of ale in local taverns, the teams often found their way back to the Fairclough stables without mishap.

When N.B. died in 1938, motor trucks had replaced the hardy teams of horses in serving the firm's wholesale and retail customers. Oil was starting to make inroads into the coal business, but John Fairclough, who had succeeded his father, was reluctant to get into the oil trade, believing it would never fully replace coal as the primary fuel.

John Homer Fairclough (1902-1950), son of N.B. Fairclough and president of the firm until his death.

Following the death of John Fairclough, Sr., in 1949, John Jr. began building the oil side of the fuel business, eventually acquiring more than 30 other companies. Today N.B. Fairclough & Son, Inc., supplies coal, gasoline, heating oil, and diesel fuel from the Hudson to the Delaware rivers, and from High Point in Sussex County to New Brunswick. The teams of horses of N.B. Fairclough's time have been supplanted by 40 trucks

John H. Fairclough, Sr. (far right), is joined by his three sons during celebration of the centennial anniversary of the firm. From left are John Lee Fairclough, Andrew N.B. Fairclough, and James Henry Fairclough.

traveling the modern highways of North Jersey.

Now known as John Sr.—following the advent of his sons, John III, James, and Andrew, into the business—he calls himself the ringmaster of a diversified corporation, including the fuel business, the 200-acre Fairview farm, and his carriages, which have become a lucrative avocation.

Fairclough attributes the firm's continued success to its commitment to superior product and service at good prices. "We seek to answer calls within 15 minutes with our radio-dispatched trucks anywhere in North Jersey," he says. "Our best advertising is word-of-mouth."

But his horses and antique carriages are his pet enterprise, one eagerly shared by his three sons. He began collecting in 1960, and now he and his sons compete in carriage-driving competitions in the United States and abroad. His carriages have participated in royal visits in this country, presidential inaugurations, and other ceremonies, as well as in promotional activities for many well-known companies. And Fairclough has no greater joy than when he takes orphans on jaunts atop his carriages, while he plays Santa. He represents the third generation of the Fairclough family to serve on the board of the Paterson Orphange.

N.B. Fairclough & Son, Inc., has witnessed many changes in the fuel business over the years. Oil replaced coal as the primary heating fuel; horses gave way to trucks. There have been fuel crises and gasoline gluts—and now even coal has reemerged as a fuel of choice in certain circumstances.

John Fairclough, Sr., says he and his sons have no plans to expand outside the North Jersey market. "This is one of the most dynamic markets in the country, with plenty of business for us," he says. "Our job is to maintain efficiency and service for our customers, just as the company has for more than 100 years."

Fairclough and his sons are, like the hard-working teams of horses of years ago, pulling together to fulfill that commitment.

In the early 1900s N.B. Fairclough & Son had a facility located adjacent to the railroad, where the company's horse-drawn wagons would load coal for delivery.

BARNERT MEMORIAL HOSPITAL CENTER

As Barnert Memorial Hospital Center nears its 80th anniversary of service to the greater Paterson community, it is truly a renewed health care institution, with newly enlarged, modern facilities and one of the most renowned staffs in the field. However, Barnert Memorial's role in serving the community began on much more modest terms.

In 1908 local Jewish and Italian doctors approached Nathan Barnert, Paterson's former mayor and leading philanthropist. They were seeking funds for a new hospital that would allow them to admit their patients, many of whom were poor immigrants. Moved by their plight, Barnert provided funds for the Miriam Barnert Memorial Dispensary, named after his late wife.

The institution opened its doors on November 29, 1908, at 56 Hamilton Avenue. It attracted many patients, and by 1910 it was necessary to relocate to larger quarters.

On January 2, 1910, the dispensary was moved to the Crosby house on Broadway and Paterson Street. It would prove to be a temporary home, for on October 12, 1913, the board of directors met with Nathan Barnert to ask for additional funds to build a full hospital facility.

That day was Nathan Barnert's 75th birthday—and he bestowed a very special birthday present on the people of Paterson and its surrounding communities. He donated $250,000, together with 16 city lots situated on Broadway between 30th and 31st streets and 13th Avenue.

This four-story hospital structure was erected between 1914 and 1916 at Barnert Memorial Hospital Center's present site.

Ground was broken in 1914 to erect a modern four-story facility at the hospital's present site, 31st Street and Broadway. The cornerstone for the newly renamed Nathan and Miriam Barnert Memorial Hospital Association was laid on October 19, 1914, with more than 5,000 marchers, representing every Jewish patriotic, religious, and service organization in the city, together with 1,500 Masons, parading before the ceremony. Bands played and people cheered on what Nathan Barnert called the happiest day

ABOVE: Another modern feature of the then-new Barnert Memorial Hospital was this motorized ambulance, circa 1916.

BELOW: This bright and airy ward was indicative of the improved care provided by Barnert Memorial Hospital's first modern building, circa 1916.

of his life.

Barnert had some definite ideas about health care and put them into the hospital's charter. In addition to requiring the institution to operate under Jewish dietary law, Barnert insisted that it "should be devoted as far as practicable to the accommodation of poor people without compensation, or with such limited compensation as they may be able to give," regardless of race, color, or creed. Barnert Memorial Hospital Center is still dedicated to those original precepts.

The hospital formally opened in 1916 with a capacity of 85 beds. Over the course of the next seven decades, through periods of war and peace, economic boom and depression, civil strife and neighborhood unity, the hospital increased the scope of its services and facilities beginning with Nathan Barnert's gift of the nurses' residence, the cornerstone of which was laid in 1924.

Four years later the operating suite was enlarged, and by the following year the hospital's capacity stood at 117 beds. A fifth floor was added in 1937, increasing the bed count to 148. Matching this physical expansion was Barnert Memorial's broadening services, including emergency rooms, children's wards, and the establishment of a blood bank.

Barnert Memorial's growth continued into the 1950s with the opening of a new wing in 1951. In addition, the institution emerged as a major teaching facility for training hospital administrators and for new physicians in such areas as pathology.

In 1954 Harvey Schoenfeld was appointed director of the hospital; he would lead Barnert Memorial over the next 30 years during its greatest expansion of services and facilities. Community health programs, including a cardiac clinic, bone and artificial graft bank, speech therapy, nutritional counseling, and prenatal programs, were initiated. All of this culminated in the dedication of Barnert Memorial Hospital Center's new building, with more than 250 beds and 30 bassinets, on November 27, 1966.

Constant upgrading and modernization has kept the hospital in the forefront of health care facilities in North Jersey.

Barnert Memorial, under the direction of president and chief executive officer Bruce M. Topolosky, stands on the threshold of a new era. An expansion program due for completion in mid-1987 will more than double the hospital's total size while adding 33 beds and providing the most modern medical technology for the people of the greater Paterson area.

Serving more than 75,000 patients per year, Barnert Memorial Hospital Center is a complete health care facility. It provides such services as toxic substance screenings; the innovative Pedia-Center, giving after-hours treatment for children; and the Mental Health Center, featuring programs in such fields as alcoholism/drug counseling, stress management, and family relationships.

Barnert Memorial Hospital Center is reaching beyond its traditional boundaries with the Corporate Health Management Network, providing businesses with health screening, executive physical examinations, and fitness programs at the work place. At the same time the institution continues to offer the surgical and medical care that has earned it a national reputation for excellence.

No greater proof of the hospital's continued commitment to the greater Paterson region can be found than the multimillion-dollar construction program nearing completion. Barnert Memorial Hospital Center is built on a foundation of medical care and community service that has prepared it for the challenges of tomorrow.

With completion slated for mid-1987, Barnert Memorial Hospital Center will undergo yet another metamorphosis to look much like this artist's rendering.

MIDLANTIC NATIONAL BANK/NORTH

On May 1, 1969, four years after the close of the Civil War and a scant two months following the inauguration of Ulysses S. Grant as President of the United States, with only 10 days until the driving of the final golden spike at Promontory Point, Utah, completing the first transcontinental railroad, the Paterson Savings Institution opened to serve working people.

Prior to that time Paterson had been served by only two banks, both commercial institutions serving businesses. A place was needed where working people could save for homes, for old age in a time when pensions and Social Security benefits were nonexistent, and for the proverbial rainy day.

Midlantic National Bank/North's modern headquarters rises above Interstate 80, overlooking Paterson, on Garret Mountain in West Paterson.

Robert Hamil, first president of the Paterson Savings Institution, Midlantic National Bank/North's earliest predecessor bank.

That first predecessor of Midlantic National Bank/North was a unique enterprise: It was the only stock-supported—rather than mutual (or depositor-owned)—savings bank east of the Mississippi. This was done to safeguard depositors in the days before federal insurance on deposits by providing $100,000 in capital for the new institution.

The first board of managers included the leading citizens of the city: manufacturers, merchants, educators, lawyers, public officials, land owners, and utilities managers. Robert Hamil of Hamil & Booth, silk manufacturers, was elected the first president with Colonel Andrew Derrom, building contractor, educator, and Civil War hero, as vice-president.

From its first location at 122 Market Street (then known as Congress Street), in quarters rented from the local gas company, Paterson Savings would evolve and grow into a major component of Midlantic Banks, Inc., a diversified bank holding company serving all of New Jersey and beyond with the most modern, broadest-based financial services available.

Over nearly 120 years what began as the Paterson Savings Institution would grow and prosper despite numerous depressions (including the Great Depression, in which it was one of the first financial institutions to reopen after the Bank Holiday of 1933), two World Wars, and innumerable crises at home and abroad. PSI and its successors provided the security and financial resources that helped engineer the growth not only of Paterson and Passaic County, but also of New Jersey and the nation.

While the Paterson Savings Insti-

The Congress Hotel was the second home of the Paterson Savings Institution. The hotel was demolished in 1892 to make way for the Paterson Savings Building located at what now is Main and Market streets.

A horse-drawn coach passes 122 Congress Street (now Market Street), the first location of Paterson Savings Institution. Photo circa 1880

The Paterson Savings Institution's office was located on the Main Street side of the Old Congress Hotel.

tution formed the taproot of today's Midlantic/North, soon after its founding other branches of the bank's "family tree" sprouted.

In Passaic, which came into its own as a manufacturing center at the end of the nineteenth century, Passaic National Bank was organized in 1886. Four years later State Trust and Safe Deposit Co., which changed its name in 1891 to the Peoples Bank and Trust Company, opened in Passaic. More than a quarter-century later, in 1925, the Clifton National Bank opened in the "new" city of Clifton, which was chartered in 1917 after being a part of the old Aquackanonk Township that predated the nation's independence.

Those four Passaic County-based financial institutions—Paterson Savings Institution, Passaic National Bank, Peoples Bank & Trust Company, and Clifton National Bank—would eventually come together to form New Jersey Bank (National Association). That entity would finally become one of the two partners forming Midlantic National Bank/North.

During the first four decades of the twentieth century the four banks grew in assets and deposits along with the area. With the primitive communications capabilities of the day branch banking, as we know it today, was impossible.

Because of the Depression, Passaic's Peoples Bank and Trust Company absorbed the American Trust Co., which itself was an amalgam of smaller banks in Passaic. The institution's "skyscraper" at 663 Main Avenue in Passaic still dominates the city's downtown shopping area.

Paterson Savings expanded in sheer physical size from its headquarters building constructed in 1892 at the corner of Main and Market streets by erecting an additional building so the bank covered the entire block on Market Street form Main to Washington.

Following World War II the savings institution's management and board recognized the need to broaden PSI's capabilities. In 1947 Paterson Savings' charter was changed to allow its entry into commercial banking, and the name became Paterson Savings & Trust Company. That same year Paterson Savings & Trust acquired 64 percent of the stock of Peoples Bank & Trust of Passaic. Four years later they formally combined as the County Bank & Trust Company.

Passaic National Bank absorbed its affiliate, Passaic Trust & Safe Deposit Co., in 1922, the same year it erected a new six-story structure at the intersection of Main Avenue and Bloomfield Avenue (now Broadway). That building, at 657 Main Avenue, is home to Midlantic/North's principal Passaic office. With the Passaic Trust merger, the institution adopted the name Passaic National Bank & Trust Company.

In 1949 Passaic National Bank & Trust joined with the Clifton National Bank, headquartered at 1184 Main Avenue in Clifton, to form the

The Passaic National Bank erected this building at the corner of Main and Bloomfield avenues (now Broadway) in 1890. The building later gave way to a new structure in 1922 where Midlantic National Bank/North's Passaic office is now located.

Passaic-Clifton National Bank & Trust Company. County Bank & Trust Company (the combination of Paterson Savings & Trust with Peoples Bank & Trust of Passaic) and the Passaic-Clifton National Bank & Trust Company merged in 1958 to form New Jersey Bank & Trust Company, which evolved eleven years later into New Jersey Bank (National Association).

The new banking organization had three headquarters: the main buildings in Paterson and Passaic as operating centers and 1184 Main Avenue in Clifton as the corporate home office. This three-way split was resolved in 1974 with the opening of the modern nine-story headquarters on Garret Mountain in West Paterson overlooking Paterson, the bank's first city of origin, and Interstate 80, which links the more than 50 branches with which Midlantic/North serves Morris, Passaic, Bergen, Essex, and Hudson counties.

Through acquisitions and new branches, New Jersey Bank served Paterson with facilities at its original 129 Market Street site, as well as at Park Avenue and 33rd Street, 31st Street and Market Avenue, and Main Street and Crooks Avenue, in addition to 17 other offices in Passaic, Clifton, West Paterson, Little Falls, Wayne, Haledon, and North Haledon.

Those branch locations in Paterson and other Passaic County communities represented more than places where the bank did business. They provided then—as they still do—a direct outreach into those communities that translated into comprehensive and innovative banking services and programs to enhance local neighborhoods.

The Paterson Savings Institution, constructed at the intersection of Main and Market streets in 1892 (site of the old Congress Hall), is shown here during the 1920s. Paterson's City Hall rises at the right. The P.S.I. building, one of the few fireproof structures in Paterson's downtown at the turn of the century, halted the progress of the Paterson fire in February 1902.

With banking law liberalization in 1969, New Jersey Bank began to expand outside Passaic County, first into Bergen, then into Morris, Essex, and Hudson counties. The institution formed a holding company, Greater Jersey Bancorp., allowing expansion into related service areas.

With the tremendous increase in the complexity of individual and business financial services as the twenty-first century approaches, and requirements for capital resources needed to accommodate them, New Jersey Bank joined Midlantic Banks, Inc., in 1983. Under the Midlantic system, which originated with the state's oldest bank (begun in 1804), New Jersey Bank joined with Midlantic/Citizens of Englewood to form Midlantic National Bank/North in 1984.

Midlantic/North brings the resources of Midlantic Banks, Inc., together with the innovation of New Jersey Bank's antecedents. Those earlier institutions introduced such novel services (for their time) as drive-in banking, automatic teller machines, consumer credit loans, international banking, personalized checking accounts, and other services that are now considered commonplace.

Midlantic National Bank/North, extending back through New Jersey Bank and its earliest predecessors, has provided the services and financial support to individuals, businesses, and municipalities of Passaic County that have earned accolades from throughout its service area and within the banking profession. Midlantic/North is not merely poised to serve. Instead it actively serves Paterson and Passaic County with resources the earlier banks could not approach, and with services they would not have imagined.

Passaic National Bank's headquarters, opened in 1922, is shown next to the construction site for the Peoples Bank & Trust Company at 663 Main Avenue. The Passaic National Bank building is now the location for Midlantic National Bank/North's Passaic office.

THE MALQUI AGENCY INC.

The history of America is filled with stories of those seeking the tremendous opportunities this country offers. Tales from the past are legion about energetic, enterprising immigrants who came to the United States and succeeded. That process is being continued today by men and women committed to making their own way and willing to take the risks success demands. Julio C. Malqui, founder and president of The Malqui Agency Inc. of Paterson, is one of those new immigrants.

In 1971, at the age of 22, Malqui left his home in Peru to come to a strange land. He arrived in Paterson and worked as a machine operator for the John Royle & Son Company. Then he enrolled at William Paterson College of New Jersey, where he majored in business administration.

While attending college he worked as a stocker for Sears, Roebuck and Co. in Wayne. Finishing his degree in three years, Malqui, who had sold everything from appliances to encyclopedias in Peru, joined Metropolitan Life Insurance Company as a sales management trainee.

After a few years with Metropolitan Life, Malqui's drive and enthusiasm pushed him to set out on his own as an independent insurance broker. Reflecting on that time, he says: "I knew my market. Nearly 90 percent of my first customers were, like myself, Spanish-speaking immigrants. (Now it is 60-percent Spanish and 40-percent American.) I understood their concerns about a new country from first-hand experience. Yes, they needed auto and life insurance and other coverage like everyone else, but they also needed someone who could help with translations and taxes and all the confusing details of everyday life in the United States. I gave them that, and won customers."

By the end of 1977, its first year in business, Julio Malqui's agency—himself and two clerical workers—had more than 2,000 clients. The company emphasized then, as it does now, full service for patrons including all forms of insurance as well as tax preparation, notary, translation, and letter-writing services. "You have to give people what they need, my business is solidly based on a 10-year tradition of good and responsible service," says Malqui.

The proof is in the performance, as demonstrated by the agency's consistent growth each year with its base now reaching more than 12,000 clients, divided evenly between the Hispanic and non-Hispanic markets. The Malqui Agency Inc. and its travel affiliate, International United Services, now employ 16 people.

Remarking about his client base, Malqui says that the majority of policies are personal life and casualty insurance, while insuring small businesses, such as local merchants, service stations, and professionals, is a growing market.

Julio C. Malqui, founder and president of The Malqui Agency Inc.

Malqui purchased the International United Services Agency of Passaic to provide travel services. Moving the travel agency to his original location at 295 Park Avenue in Paterson, Malqui relocated his insurance agency next door. "Many of my clients still have families outside the country," he says. "The bulk of our business is arranging air passage, although we do offer package vacation plans as well. It is a well-rounded, travel agency."

Ten years after going into business, Julio Malqui still works hard and puts in long hours. "We're building for the future," he says.

PROSPECT PARK SAVINGS AND LOAN ASSOCIATION

From left: Doris Misner, Theodore Bruinsma, and Margretta Veenstra Van Dyke in front of the original Prospect Park Building and Loan Association office.

The year 1986 marked Prospect Park Savings and Loan Association's 60th year of service to Passaic County. Those decades witnessed many changes in the local area, in services being offered by financial institutions, and in directions being taken by those institutions. Much has changed, but Prospect Park Savings and Loan's commitment to integrity and a sense of responsibility for the financial well-being of its customers remains the same today as it was 60 years ago.

Thrift was a household byword in the Prospect Park Borough of the mid-1920s. Those in the borough who began to prosper had a strong desire to help their neighbors, and on February 24, 1926, thirteen business and civic leaders laid the groundwork for the Prospect Park Building and Loan Association.

The first officers of the organization were Frank P. Stagg, president; Cornelius Van Vlaanderen, vice-president; Harry J. Van Hook, treasurer; and Theodore "Chet" Bruinsma, secretary, a post he held until becoming president in 1962. He was named to the post of chairman in 1974. Now chairman emeritus, Bruinsma had served the association for its entire history.

Bruinsma was the very personification of the values upon which the organization was founded. He demonstrated his love for his community by his dedicated service as an elected official, business leader, and officer of the association.

After operating for a short time in a local commercial bank, the organization moved to space in Bruinsma's insurance agency at 130 Haledon Avenue. Growth brought Prospect Park Savings and Loan Association to its first separate location in 1961, a storefront in a nearby Haledon shopping center. Three years later Russell L. Frignoca joined the board of directors and was named executive vice-president and managing officer in 1968. Now president, chairman, and chief executive officer, Frignoca has led the organization through its greatest period of growth and diversification.

The 1970s saw Prospect Park Savings and Loan expand into new facilities. Today the association has a total of four banking offices: two in Haledon, one in Totowa, and an office in its West Paterson corporate headquarters.

With physical expansion came a broadening of services, including auto, personal, home improvement, and student loans; interest-bearing checking (N.O.W.) accounts; and other services. In addition, Prospect Park Savings and Loan formed subsidiaries providing new fields of income and service. They include real estate acquisition, development, and sales; joint ventures with professional builders; low-cost life insurance; and annuities. Today the association is a full-service community financial center providing services that range from discount brokerage to commercial loans.

In 1983 a Prospect Park Savings subsidiary, West Meadow Realty, completed the first mixed-use professional/commercial condominium center in the eastern United States. The administrative headquarters of the association is based in that complex.

Prospect Park Savings and Loan Association has grown and matured in the past 60 years, and the example of dedicated service set by Theodore Bruinsma is still being followed by its officers and staff in serving the needs of its home communities.

The modern administrative headquarters of Prospect Park Savings and Loan Association in West Paterson.

WESTMONT HOME

In 1881 the Ryerson Homestead served as a residence for the elderly women of Paterson, and was the predecessor of the Westmont Home.

Paterson is the site of a piece of living history—the Westmont Home, a residence with roots that are directly connected to the city's silken past. Now a residential health care facility, the Westmont Home traces its origins to the Old Ladies Home of Paterson, founded in 1875.

The home was started by businessmen who saw the need for a home for the elderly women who had taught their children, worked in their mills and homes, and who had no one to care for them. Robert Hamil, of Hamil & Booth, silk manufacturers, and the first president of the Paterson Savings Institution (from which the present Midlantic National Bank/North grew), was the facility's first president. The home was located in the Carrick House on York Avenue and accommodated 19 ladies.

By 1881 the Carrick House proved too small for all those applying for residence. John Dunlop, the second president of the home, purchased the Ryerson Homestead, at what is now 265 Totowa Avenue near the Great Falls, for $5,400, and the home relocated to its permanent site.

At first the board of directors was composed entirely of men, but beginning in 1881 a board of women was organized in response to the needs of the residents. The first important assignment for the "assistant lady managers" was to prepare the new home for occupancy and transfer the residents.

In 1887 the change from the original Board of Gentlemen Governors to Lady Managers was effected. Women have served on the board exclusively ever since. The board calls on the advisory board, which includes both men and women, for special needs.

During the past century leading women of Paterson selflessly served the residents of the home. Many were the wives of prominent businessmen, such as Mrs. Garret A. Hobart, whose husband later became Vice-President of the United States, and Mrs. Frederick W. Cooke, whose husband was the locomotive manufacturer. Each of these women, remarkable in her own right, served as president of the facility.

Today the Westmont Home (its name since 1962) is a vibrant "life care" facility for women—and men —over age 55. The Westmont is truly "home," with a full program of activities conducted in a warm, homelike atmosphere. Originally a residential facility only, the Westmont offers nursing care, and has embarked on such new programs as Senior Daycare, which provides temporary residential service for older adults who require attention.

The average age of the home's 39 residents is 88, with the eldest at 98 and the youngest at 72. But age is not a major factor among the residents as they enjoy a full menu of activities, including daytrips in the Westmont's van, games, movies, arts and crafts, dances, and reading and speakers groups.

The Old Ladies Home of the past has matured to become a vibrant and lively residence for those who have lived the history of Paterson and its surrounding communities.

Now a residential health care facility, the Westmont Home traces its origins to the Old Ladies Home of Paterson founded in 1875.

HETERENE CHEMICAL COMPANY, INC.

The partnership of production and sales creates a fundamental synergy in any business. Many good examples of such effective combinations exist in the greater Paterson region, and Heterene Chemical Company, Inc., is one such model for business ventures.

The firm was founded in October 1966 by Alan I. Wolpert, a Princeton-trained chemical engineer. The following year David S. Dean, Wolpert's former associate from Treplow Products in Paterson, joined him as a partner and assumed responsibility for the management of the new enterprise. Together they formed a complementary team, combining optimum technical expertise with astute sales and management abilities.

Heterene Chemical Company's headquarters, situated amid a nine-building, 3.5-acre complex at 295 Vreeland Avenue.

The chemical industry has been undergoing major changes during the past three decades. Whereas the industry had been formerly dominated by a relatively few corporate giants, new techniques and products created a specialty chemical field. It is that market that Heterene Chemical Company has identified as its field of operations.

Beginning in the mid-1960s with a new manufacturing process for making nonionic surfactants or detergents, the company was able to customize certain chemical specialties for those customers seeking individual products different from mass-sale items. Today Heterene is producing unique specialities primarily for the personal care and cosmetic industries.

Manufacturers of consumer products, such as body lotions, lipsticks, shampoos, and perfumes, are major users of Heterene materials. And a new line of patented products will expand the firm's role in the cosmetics industry.

The company also produces millions of pounds of quaternary compounds used in the production of sanitizers, deodorants, germicides, and swimming pool bactericides. Truly, in its own unobtrusive way, Heterene Chemical Company manufactures many of the compounds for the products of national corporations, such as Avon, Bristol Myers, and Johnson & Johnson, that each of us uses or comes in contact with every day.

The firm has been based in Paterson since its earliest days. It has grown from its original location covering 10,000 square feet to a 3.5-acre complex of nine buildings at 295 Vreeland Avenue. In expanding Heterene Chemical's base of operations, Wolpert and Dean have organized an affiliated company, Thermo-cote, Inc., which is also located in Paterson. This new venture produces coatings used by more than 50 industries including electronics and computers. Wolpert and Dean prove that the entrepreneurial spirit still thrives in Paterson, where transportation, a sizeable labor force, and a positive business climate are readily found.

Pictured here is one of the nine buildings in which Heterene Chemical Company manufactures many of the chemical compounds that go into such consumer products as body lotions, lipsticks, shampoos, and perfumes.

GREAT FALLS VENDING CORPORATION

Paterson's location at the hub of major highway systems lends itself most effectively to highly mobile types of business enterprises. Certainly no business endeavor is more dependent upon excellent road transportation systems than the vending industry. Great Falls Vending Corporation is a prime example of the importance of the city's strategic placement to effective operations.

Great Falls Vending is a relatively new member of Paterson's business community, having been started by Richard Tanis, Jr., in 1978. However, the company's roots extend back nearly 40 years, when Tanis began in the industry with his father, Richard Sr., and brother John with Spotless Lunch Industrial Service & Vending, which served local businesses by delivering milk, doughnuts, coffee, and sandwiches from catering trucks.

By the late 1970s the technology of business luncheon and catering services had changed, and Richard Tanis, Jr., joined by his wife, Barbara Mae, daughters Barbara Jean Schell and Carolyn, son Richard, and nephew Frank Fanning launched Great Falls Vending Corporation.

The firm's seven staff members now serve vending machines offering such fare as soft drinks, juices, milk, and hot and cold sandwiches in decorated "lunch area" environments. In addition, a major part of the company's business is supplying office and factory coffee makers with coffee, tea, cups, and condiments. Great Falls Vending's centralized Crooks Avenue headquarters places its service vehicles minutes away from customer locations in the Meadowlands or the corporate campuses of Morris County, north to Mahwah, and south through Essex and Union counties.

The firm serves a diversified customer base, including hospitals, post offices, industrial facilities, and schools. The key to Great Falls Vending's success, says Tanis, is "a commitment to providing top-quality food and beverages in efficiently operating equipment."

While his business requires many hours of personal attention, including servicing his customers' needs himself, Tanis has many broad interests, including collecting military-related toys. "I specialize in post-1940 items, some are collectors items while others just interest me," he says. "Friends and relatives are always giving me things they pick up, and I frequently attend antiques and toy shows for special pieces."

In addition to his hobby, Tanis is active in the Paterson Rotary Club, but his special interest is the Paterson YMCA of which he is vice-president and residence chairman.

Richard Tanis, Jr., and his Great Falls Vending Corporation are examples of the continuing healthy environment Paterson provides for entrepreneurs as the city nears the close of its second century.

Richard Tanis, Jr., is now residing in Point Arena, California, running a restaurant. The business is now being operated by his two daughters, Barbara Jean Schell and Carolyn Tanis; his nephew, Frank Fanning; and Robert Sole.

PETER GARAFANO & SON, INC.

The company started by Peter Garafano in 1943 as a welding and repair shop is today a design, construction, and sales/service organization for the trucking industry that covers approximately the eastern half of the United States.

Peter Garafano, born in Italy, came to this country as a child, where his family settled in Paterson. He went to work early in that city's famous silk mills, but later joined the Leslie & Elliot Company, where he apprenticed and learned boiler repairs, becoming skilled at welding.

During World War II he served at the Brooklyn Navy Yard, where he helped build the famous battleships *Missouri* and *Iowa*. The skills of Garafano and his fellow workers is attested to today by the recommissioning of those great ships more than 40 years later.

Despite the long Brooklyn hours Garafano set up his own welding and repair shop next to his home on Wabash Avenue in Paterson. With metals scarce, his skills in repairing boilers and tanks were highly valued.

The three generations of the Garafano family are shown with one of the tank trailers manufactured and serviced by the company at its modern facility at the base of historic Garret Mountain. From left are Peter Garafano III, Peter Garafano, Sr., Peter Garafano, Jr., and Daniel Garafano.

After the war he pursued his new business on a full-time basis. He became a journeyman welder, traveling to his customers' locations to work on their premises.

By the early 1950s he and his son, Peter Jr., who worked with him on a part-time basis before joining the Marines, began building a full-service shop at 262-266 Wabash Avenue. Following his son's return, Garafano's business grew, and the company had five employees when it was incorporated in 1956.

In addition to the firm's welding services, Garafano and his son branched out into structural steel and ornamental ironwork. Eventually Peter Garafano & Son, Inc., began servicing fuel companies with its storage tanks, tank trucks, and fuel pipes.

A major customer was Boulevard Fuel Oil, whose needs helped the Garafano operation evolve into a tank and tank truck specialist. When Hess Oil acquired Boulevard, Garafano's business increased dramatically, and its staff rose to 15 people.

The shop on Wabash Avenue was expanded in 1970 to three bays, but with customers such as Exxon, Shotmeyer Brothers, Oil City, and dozens of independent oil distributors, Peter Jr., who had assumed control of operations, sought to expand facilities. With support from city officials, the firm was able to acquire a three-acre site on Marshall Street, where a 12-bay facility was opened in 1981.

Peter Garafano & Son, Inc., has always been a family business. First it was the father and son. Then Peter Jr.'s wife, Eleanor, became an active member in the firm when she managed the company books and handled business matters from an office in her home. Now Peter Jr. is joined by the third generation of the Garafano family, with sons Peter III and Daniel coming into the business.

The firm currently has two divisions: Garafano Tank Service, which sells and services tank trucks and trailers for customers from Boston to Louisiana; and Steelfab, acquired in 1984, which manufactures dump truck bodies, hoists, and other heavy equipment and has distributors throughout the Northeast.

According to Peter Jr., Paterson has been crucial to the firm's success due to the city's strategic location and the assistance of local officials. With those advantages and the firm's flexible approach to the marketplace, Peter Garafano & Son, Inc., is a company looking forward.

Three generations of the Garafano family have operated Peter Garafano & Son, Inc., located at 500 Marshall Street. Pictured here are (left to right) Peter Garafano, Sr., founder of the company; Peter Garafano, Jr., president; Daniel Garafano; and Peter Garafano III (rear).

THERMWELL PRODUCTS CO., INC.

The ability of businesses to evolve distinguishes those firms that continue in existence from the multitudes that fall. Paterson's Thermwell Products Co., Inc., is such a business that has set itself apart as one of the true success stories of the old Silk City. The common thread of immigrant vision and determination that is woven through the tapestries of other companies' histories binds together the roots of Thermwell today.

Founded as the Thermwool Company in 1910 by Russian immigrant brothers, Frank and Harry Gerstein, the enterprise first produced felt carpet. Located in New York City, the operation moved to Newark during the 1940s before finally settling in Paterson in the 1950s. In existence now more than three-quarters of a century, Thermwell Products Co., Inc., has its headquarters and three production plants in Paterson.

Today the pioneer of consumer weather-related products serves a nationwide market with an unsurpassed selection of more than 2,000 insulation-related products under Thermwell's own Frost-King label, as well as manufacturing for other marketers' private labels.

The company broadened its original base by manufacturing weather-stripping products under the Frost-King line during the early 1960s. In 1967 Thermwell was acquired by Frank and Harry Gerstein's three sons: David, who is president of the company; Irving, executive vice-president; and Mel, secretary/treasurer.

The brothers' acquisition marked Thermwell's aggressive expansion program that continues today. Acquired were Regent Tape Company of Boston, producer of masking tape; Kraver Screen Company of Miami, producers of window screening; Gering Products of Kenilworth, producer of plastic runners; Mortell, Inc., of Chicago, Illinois, manufacturer of Mortite Caulk; and Eagle Lamp Company, manufacturer of Eagle Hurricane Lamps and scented oil. These acquisitions fit well with Thermwell's entry in the do-it-yourself market.

In addition to its acquisitions, Thermwell also organized Filmco Industries, Inc., which produces plastic sheeting and garbage bags, and at present is still operating Lever Manufacturing Corporation (slitting equipment and brazing machinery).

The company has sales offices in every state and markets to Canada and Europe. Thermwell manufacturing plants are also located in California, Illinois, and Georgia, with major East and West Coast distribution centers in Mahwah and Los Angeles, respectively. The firm employs 1,000 people nationwide, with 300 persons working in Paterson alone.

Mel Gerstein notes that Thermwell's plan is to broaden its scope and strengthen its position as the leading manufacturer and marketer of packaged weather stripping and insulation. "Paterson provides us with an excellent operating base," says Gerstein. "The business environment here has all that we need—good labor market and excellent transportation facilities."

Thermwell Products Co., Inc., and its Frost-King line of products help keep Paterson's manufacturing heritage alive—and serve consumers' needs through a ubiquitous presence in hardware stores and home centers across the country.

THE WOOD PRESS, INC.

Located on East 41st Street near Route 20 and Interstate 80, The Wood Press, Inc., is the largest printing company in the city. Founded in 1915 by Robert E. Wood, Jr., the firm employs 75 people and occupies a 44,000-square-foot plant.

The business was started by Robert E. Wood, Jr., in the basement of a home in Athenia. In 1916 Wood built the first plant in the Athenia section of Clifton. The local post office (with Wood as postmaster) occupied the front, and the print shop was located in the back.

While Wood served in the Army as a second lieutenant during World War I, the printing business lapsed. In the meantime Wood's wife, Ada, became assistant postmaster and ran the Athenia branch. Upon his return from service, Wood resumed his position as postmaster and rekindled the printing business. His income from the postal position paid the family's living expenses, while earnings from the printing operation were channeled back into the business.

The company's final relocation, to its present site on East 41st Street, took place in 1953. Today The Wood Press, Inc., is one of the leading suppliers of graphic arts and printing services in the Tri-State area, with customers from New England to Washington, D.C.

In 1925 the company moved to larger quarters on Clifton Avenue in Clifton. Three years later Wood merged with Glover Press under the name Glover-Wood Press, with a plant located at 10 Mill Street in Paterson using steam generated by S.U.M. from the Passaic Falls for heating. Within a year Wood purchased his partner's share, and Wood Press was incorporated. The company continued to grow, serving diverse manufacturing, retail, and commercial customers in the Paterson region. During World War II Wood Press moved to a new site at 2-18 River Street. In 1946 Robert E. Wood, Jr., passed away. His son, Robert III, newly discharged as a naval officer, succeeded him in managing the growing business.

The company's final relocation, to its present site, took place in 1953. Subsequent expansions have made Wood Press one of the leading suppliers of graphic arts and printing services in the Tri-State area, with customers from New England to Washington, D.C. Today corporate operations are directed by Robert H. "Bert" Wood, president, while Robert E. Wood III serves as chairman and chief executive officer. Sales have grown from $125,000 in 1946 to more than $10 million in 1985.

The Wood Press, Inc., was founded in 1915 by Robert E. Wood, Jr., pictured here.

Forty years ago letterpresses printed single-side, one-color sheets at a rate of 1,000 to 2,500 per hour. Now the firm's newest web lithographic press, at a cost of two million dollars, prints five colors at 40,000 sheets per hour on both sides. Customers include financial institutions, regional businesses, and *Fortune* 500 companies. The firm produces pharmaceutical labels and inserts, catalogues, brochures, direct mail, and annual reports—almost all in multicolor.

The Wood Press, Inc., remains another example of Paterson's leadership in products and services to businesses and consumers throughout the Northeast and the nation.

Robert E. Wood III (left), son of founder Robert E. Wood, Jr., succeeded his father in managing the company in 1946, when the elder Wood passed away. Today corporate operations are directed by Robert H. "Bert" Wood (right), and Robert E. Wood III serves as chairman and chief executive officer of the company.

AUTO EQUIPMENT, INC.

During the 1940s the firm became a major servicer for military vehicles as well as for buses for public transportation. Another change came in the 1940s, when Zachary moved the company to its present site in Paterson. This photo of the Auto Equipment shop on Market Street was taken at that time, although it still looks the same today.

Irving Zachary is a senior statesman of the truck aftermarket. Now in his nineties, Zachary was there at the advent of many innovations in truck equipment taken for granted today. The progression from Zachary's days as a service station owner in Passaic to a leading truck equipment distributor began in the early years of this century. Zachary was one of that vast flood of humanity flowing into the United States.

His start in the New World was not easy for the young Russian émigré. His father was a rabbi who struggled to support 18 sons and daughters. The determination of the father passed to the son, who by the early 1920s opened an auto service station in Passaic.

However, pumping gasoline and car repairs were not Zachary's sole occupations. Rather he built on those aspects of the business. He became a leading dealer of Goodyear tires, just as the industry evolved from solid to pneumatic tires.

By the 1930s most of his business involved trucks, especially the installation of air brakes. In those days air brakes were not standard equipment. Instead, trucks used hydraulic braking systems similar to those found on cars but less efficient for the larger vehicles. Auto Equipment, Inc., established a market for itself by retrofitting trucks with Westinghouse air brakes, or upgrading trucks' existing hydraulic systems with Bendix vacuum boosters.

Irving Zachary, a Russian émigré, founded Auto Equipment, Inc., in the early 1920s in Passaic.

Changes in truck servicing in the 1930s, coupled with the Great Depression, made any business a struggle. But Irving Zachary persevered. Later he would joke that he enjoyed the Depression because he "didn't jump out a window," but beneath the levity was arduous effort. Auto Equipment, Inc., survived because of the principles of Irving Zachary, whose business philosophy can be summed up as: "Don't borrow money, pay your bills (and don't miss discounts), and keep your word."

During World War II Auto Equipment became a major servicer for military vehicles. Zachary's mechanics were on the road from Newburgh, New York, to Atlantic City, working on Army trucks, as well as buses for public transportation.

The war was not the only change to occur in the 1940s, as Zachary moved his firm to its present site in Paterson. Paterson's appeal today is the same as then—good labor base and excellent access to the company's markets throughout the Tri-State area and beyond.

The scope of the business has changed from repairs to equipment distribution. Today Auto Equipment, Inc., services and installs top brand truck equipment such as Bendix-Westinghouse air brakes, "fifth wheel" trailer assemblies, and other vital components. Zachary's Auto Equipment, Inc., based in Paterson, helps keep America rolling.

BRAGG FUNERAL HOMES, INC.

There are many family-owned businesses in the greater Paterson area. These enterprises have been passed down, often through multiple generations. In each case, that original seed of inspiration that brought about the creation and growth of a company —whether it be a neighborhood grocery or a major manufacturing plant—is reflected in the continuing care and stewardship of business management. In rare instances much more than a sound capital structure and ample customer base is passed from one generation to its successors in a family business.

At times succeeding generations in a family business will have a broader viewpoint and wider understanding of the economic and social concerns of people—whether in a city such as Paterson or in some rural farming community. That ability to recognize the greater issues surrounding businesses and individuals and to act on them—while maintaining the viability of the business enterprise—is a rare gift. During the modern history of Paterson there has been a small number of individuals who have come forward to accept the challenge of their times, and who have passed on a legacy of service and commitment to the city, its people, and surrounding communities.

Carnie P. Bragg, Sr., founder of Bragg Funeral Homes, Inc., was such a man. Nearly 15 years after his untimely death, his devotion to civic duty as well as his astute business practices provide the foundation on which his son, Carnie Jr., now president of Bragg Funeral Homes, builds the structure for changing social and economic conditions.

At the beginning prospects for Carnie Bragg, Sr., were as limited as they were for most blacks during the 1920s and 1930s. Born in Port Chester, New York, his mother was a cook, and his father pursued one of the few options for earning more than a subsistence wage—he was a bootlegger during Prohibition.

At the age of 13 young Carnie began working in the locker room of a segregated country club in Greenwich, Connecticut. Years later, in a different social environment and certainly in a different economic situation, Bragg took great enjoyment in playing the links of that same country club.

Despite his natural intelligence and ambition, Bragg worked in those menial positions not closed to him because of his race following graduation from high school. After working as a trash collector in Connecticut, he began working for a funeral home in Stamford. This became the turning point of Bragg's professional life. He went on to attend the ReNouard School of Embalming in New York City, and was apprenticed at the Robert Cotten Funeral Home in Montclair, New Jersey.

In 1937, at the age of 24, Carnie Bragg, Sr., established his own funeral home at 143 Myrtle Avenue in Passaic. The building was a storefront in which wakes and funerals were conducted. Preparation of the dead was done in the basement, while Bragg's family resided in back rooms.

In keeping with the restrictions of the day, Bragg's clientele were black families residing in the Passaic area. By 1945 the business had grown sufficiently for Bragg to seek broader opportunities, and he opened a second funeral home that year at 256 Graham Avenue (now Rosa Parks Boulevard). Because of laws governing funeral directors' business, Bragg was the licensed mortician for the Passaic branch, while his wife, Eunice, ran the Paterson operation.

In spite of his Paterson business' slow start, Bragg's civic and political interests grew. He ultimately served on the board of the first nursery for working mothers in Passaic (The Guidance Guild). He was also active with the chamber of commerce, the Boys Club, Broadway Bank & Trust, and served as commissioner of Paterson's board of public works. In addition, he was an unsuccessful candidate for the state senate in 1948.

Bragg's stature as a committed civic leader and successful businessman continued to grow during the 1950s and 1960s. He was especially well known for his speaking ability, which frequently led to his work as a master of ceremonies for local groups.

Bragg's son, Carnie Jr., began working for the business on a part-time basis after school during this period. By the time he graduated from Fisk University in 1961 and served in the National Guard, Carnie Jr. was being prepared to take over the reins of the company, with the support of the senior Bragg's brother, George, who also worked in the family business.

The funeral home grew. But with his son's assistance and a growing staff, Carnie Bragg, Sr., had greater opportunity to serve the civic needs of the city. He also became more active in professional organizations, serving as president of a funeral directors' trade association. Carnie Bragg, Sr., was at the zenith of his professional and civic careers when he was killed in an automobile accident in 1972.

With his father's passing, Carnie Jr. took over the seat on the board of directors of Broadway Bank & Trust. The son has also succeeded his father on the board of the chamber, as a past president of Rotary, and as a participant in other worthwhile activities.

Carnie Bragg's wife, Marlene, is the newest member of the family to join the firm. A graduate of Mercer County Community College in West Windsor, New Jersey, she received her license in 1985.

The Bragg Funeral Homes are well known for fair prices and special attention to individuals and families bereft of loved ones. Honesty and caring were standards set by Carnie Bragg, Sr., that have stood the test of time.

The late Carnie P. Bragg, Sr., founder of Bragg Funeral Homes, Inc.

NEW JERSEY BELL

Although the telephone emerged in Passaic County only a few years after its invention, it didn't exactly set the world on fire. Only 11 customers had signed up for service when the first telephone exchange opened in Paterson on Christmas Eve, 1879. In those days few realized the potential of telecommunications and regarded the new telephone gadget as nothing more than a rich man's toy.

The first Passaic County exchange, located at the corner of Main and Ellison streets, was described by one reporter as a "wilderness of wires, batteries, signals, and magnets." The exchange was founded by John F. Noonan, who is considered the "father of telecommunications" in the Passaic/Bergen area.

In June 1881 he opened a second exchange in the City of Passaic with 19 customers. A year later service in the area was taken over by the New York and New Jersey Telephone Company, which operated until it became part of the New York Telephone Company in 1909.

In 1885 the telephone exchange in Paterson was moved to larger quarters on the third floor of the Blue Front Building at 207 Main Street. In 1900 Paterson's first telephone company-owned building was opened at 170 Paterson Street and housed the state's first common-battery switchboard. This technological advance did away with the old crank-style wooden telephones.

In the years that followed demand for telephone service increased dramatically. New Jersey Bell, incorporated in 1927, continued to meet the growing demand by expanding and modernizing the telecommunications network. Today 300,000 customers are served by modern switching facilities in Passaic, Paterson, Clifton, Haledon, Little Falls, Mountain View, Pompton Lakes, Erskine Lakes, West Milford, and Newfoundland.

All areas, except the Newfoundland exchange, are served by state-of-the-art Electronic Switching System (ESS) facilities. Newfoundland is scheduled for ESS conversion in 1988. With ESS, premium services, such as Call Forwarding, Call Waiting, Three-Way Calling, and two-digit Speed Calling, are available to customers.

New Jersey Bell also is meeting the growing needs of its business customers by providing efficient and economical high-technology services.

Centrex III, for example, provides small to large business customers with a low-cost and flexible alternative to expensive private branch exchange and key telecommunications systems. Customers are able to substantially reduce overhead costs because Centrex systems are located in New Jersey Bell switching offices.

New Jersey Bell's new Public Data Network (PDN) service also is helping business customers move data more accurately and economically. With PDN, computers, personal computers, and terminals of all types and sizes can communicate with error-free reliability.

The installation of new fiber-optic transmission facilities also is helping to improve the quality of voice, data, and video communications.

In addition to the quality of service provided to Passaic County customers, New Jersey Bell also has a substantial economic impact in the area. The company provides jobs for nearly 1,000 people in the county, maintains 25 corporate locations in 10 Passaic municipalities, and, in 1985, paid almost seven million dollars in property and franchise taxes.

The first telephone exchange in Passaic County was located on the third floor of the old Clark building on the corner of Main and Ellison streets. The Paterson Telephone Exchange opened for business on December 24, 1879, three years after Alexander Graham Bell invented the telephone.

Modern Electronic Switching Systems (ESS), like the one below, are serving Passaic County customers in the Little Falls and Mountain View exchange areas. All Passaic County customers will be served by ESS by the end of 1988.

BRAWER BROS., INC.

Brawer Bros., Inc., headquartered in Haledon, traces its origins to two great influences in the development of Paterson: migrations from eastern Europe and Paterson's emergence as the Silk City.

Arthur Brawer was one of five brothers who emigrated to the United States from Latvia in 1900. Arthur's ambition was to own a textile business, and he settled in Paterson, then known as the Silk City of America.

In 1903, with $2,500 of his own savings and borrowed money, Arthur Brawer launched the A. Brawer Silk Company. He planned to purchase silk yarn from excess production of silk processors at a reduced price, and sell this silk to weavers in Paterson. Processors now had a place to sell excess silk yarn, and weavers had a source for economical silk supplies.

By 1912 Brawer had acquired a processing plant on River Street in Paterson and began processing raw silk into weavable yarn. Later he added a plant in Scranton, Pennsylvania. In 1920 Arthur Brawer converted his business into a new company, Brawer Bros. Silk Company, with each of the five brothers as equal stockholders. Louis was in charge of manufacturing, the younger brothers—David, Abram, and Samuel—went into sales, while Arthur provided overall management.

The firm took a bold step during the Roaring Twenties by shifting from the processing and sale of silk yarn to the processing and sale of "artificial silk," produced by Du Pont and later known as rayon. Man-made fibers carried the company through the Depression years. Today Du Pont continues as the firm's largest supplier. Brawer Bros. added a new dimension in 1930 with the introduction of dyeing for man-made fibers.

The Depression years, followed by World War II, represented a difficult period for the company. The sluggish markets of the 1930s forced Brawer Bros. to cut profit margins to the bone. World War II and its rationing by allotment limited the firm's production ability.

Arthur Brawer died in 1946, followed by his brothers soon after. Management of the company—now called Brawer Bros., Inc.—passed to Arthur's son, Irving, an attorney, who joined the business in 1941. Despite serious difficulties during the late 1940s and early 1950s, Brawer Bros, Inc., under Irving was directed to increasingly more sophisticated technology, and additional plants were opened in Pennsylvania.

Today the company's main office is still located near Paterson, with four plants in Pennsylvania. The third generation of the Brawer family, led by Irving's nephew Charles as president, is emerging as leaders of Brawer Bros., Inc., in developing new products, markets, and technology to confront the challenges of the future.

A portrait of Arthur Brawer, a Latvian immigrant who founded, in 1903, the company that would become Brawer Bros., Inc.

PIKE CONSTRUCTION CO.

Paul H. Abrams and Isaac N. "Ike" Weiner, the sole stockholders and founders of Pike Construction Co., are lifelong friends. Ever since attending Paterson schools together, Abrams and Weiner have been a team. And for more than a quarter-century that team has brought Pike Construction Co. (Pike is a derivation of their first names) to the fore as one of the most successful and reputable general contractors in New Jersey.

Formed in 1958 when the two partners were in their early twenties, Pike Construction Co. has been commissioned for all types of general construction work. The firm's diversified portfolio includes senior citizen housing such as Paterson's Maurice Brick Apartments (converted from the century-old Little Sisters of the Poor Home); educational structures such as Jefferson Township Junior-Senior High School; shopping malls, including the K mart Plaza in Randolph Township; industrial projects such as Sealy Mattress Co. in Paterson; YM-YWHA of North Jersey in Wayne; parking garages; and a host of other specialized structures.

Whether for the public or private sector, Pike Construction Co. has established a record for on-time completion. The secret of its success, says Weiner, is planning and a willingness on the part of the two principals to become deeply involved in each project. "Each of us takes management responsibility, respectively, for the company's projects," he notes. "Paul may take the lead on one project with me backing up, and vice versa. In this way we can keep a direct handle on all activities."

The Pike organization consists of licensed engineers, architects, and other technically skilled individuals. The firm provides all supervision, technology, and backup for any project.

From its first project—the renovation of a dry cleaning shop—to major undertakings, such as Passaic County's tallest building, the 21-story Governor Paterson Tower III, Pike Construction's success has been based on uncompromising quality combined with a sense of adventure. "You never do the same things continually in this business," stated Abrams. "It's not the kind of job that is boring."

Weiner points with pride to renovation and restoration projects the company has undertaken in renewing Paterson's historical district. "We have helped turn jewels of another era—a time when this city was making its mark in everything from locomotive manufacturing to silk—to useful and truly beautiful housing. Our work has given new life to reminders of our past," he says.

Pike Construction Co. has built a reputation for integrity, reliability, and professional competence. The firm has erected housing, health care facilities, industrial plants, and schools, and is helping Paterson build a future on the foundations of the past.

Paul Abrams and Ike Weiner are truly Partners in Progress.

The Governor Paterson Tower III, located in Paterson, is the tallest building in Passaic County. It was constructed for the Riese Corporation to provide housing for older adults.

Paul Abrams (left) and Isaac Weiner (right) are the founders and principals of Pike Construction Co.

A recently completed Pike Construction Co. project is this facility for Sealy Mattress Company.

POWER BATTERY COMPANY, INC.

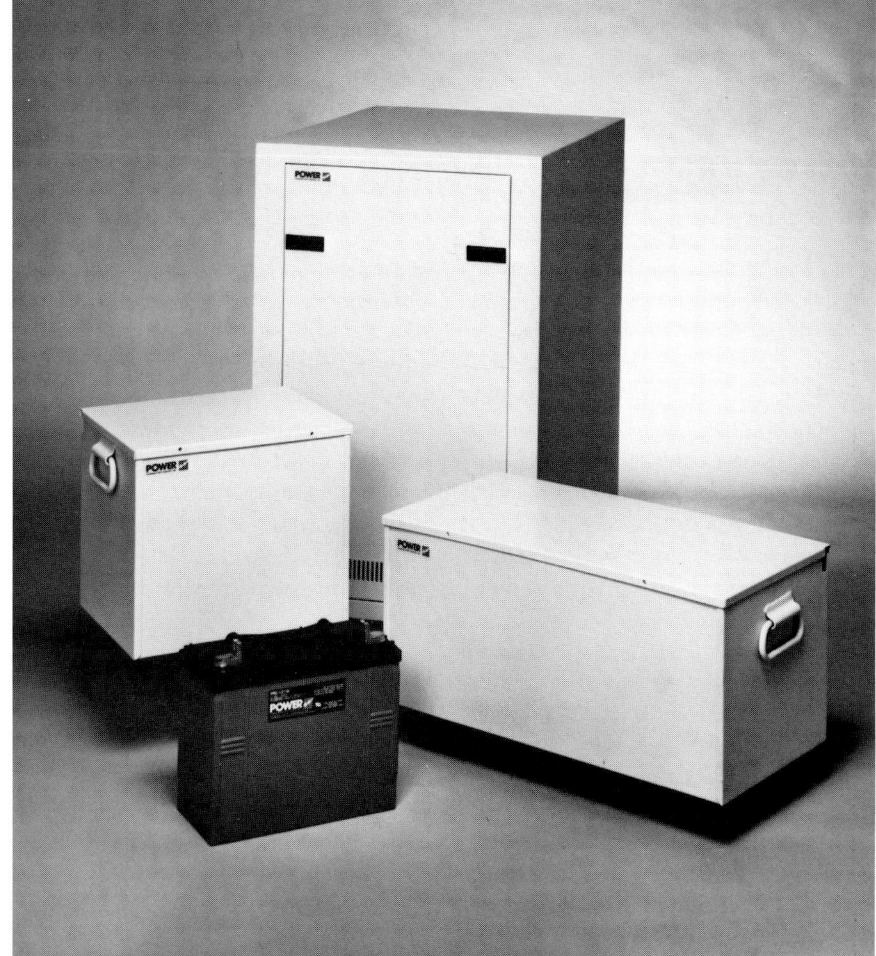

Pictured here are some of the firm's battery cabinet systems, along with the Power PRC 12110 Battery.

Computer centers for federal, state, and local government agencies; NASA; major companies; and others require uninterrupted electrical power. A major source for the large-capacity storage batteries for these systems is found on East 42nd Street in Paterson.

Power Battery Company, Inc., is a relatively new business, having been founded by William Rasmussen in 1972. While the organization is young, its roots date back to the 1930s, when Atlantic Battery Company was established by Rasmussen's great uncle, Charles Stoudt.

Atlantic Battery, now a sister company with Power Battery, manufactures plates and lead components for battery manufacturers. The business was taken over by Rasmussen's father, Ralph, in 1946. It became headquartered in Paterson during the early 1970s.

Bill Rasmussen worked with his father at Atlantic Battery, producing high-quality components for heavy-equipment battery manufacturers. He began marketing batteries on a part-time basis in 1972, going to full time a year later.

At first Power Battery rented space from Atlantic Battery on East 42nd Street and leased a warehouse on Market Street. In the beginning the company dealt with truck and heavy construction equipment batteries. Then the firm began providing batteries for major emergency lighting needs in buildings and other facilities.

With the large-scale expansion of computers in business, government, and other applications, Power Battery began producing large-capacity stationary storage batteries used by major computer centers to ensure uninterrupted power. "Even a brief shutdown of computers can cause irreparable losses," says Rasmussen. "Our batteries are integral components in emergency power systems to safeguard against such eventualities."

As specialists in computer-support battery applications, Power Battery has been expanding dramatically since its inception. From its original location in the Atlantic Battery facility at 546 East 42nd Street, the company has expanded to include all of 543-553 East 42nd Street. In addition, the firm purchased the Leschel Buick building, where Rasmussen is expanding into the truck and auto parts business, a line he first introduced in 1979 in connection with the truck battery business.

Rasmussen describes his business location in glowing terms, citing its strategic position, ample labor supply, responsive government, and excellent police and fire departments. "I really can't say enough about the police and fire departments," says Rasmussen. "They are really top-shelf."

This is the age of the computer. Power Battery Company, Inc., is building on the essential backup power needs of those all-encompassing pieces of machinery to position itself for new challenges and greater growth in the future.

Power Battery's brand-new auto and truck parts store.

MORNINGSIDE GREENHOUSE

Brian Fischer says he has been at his family's business, Morningside Greenhouse, located on West Broadway in Haledon, for 41 years and nine months. The 41 years constitute his age, while the nine months cover the time his mother, Ruth, carried him as she worked with her husband, Benjamin, who started the business in 1937.

The Fischers are a close-knit family whose business abounds with brothers and their wives, a sister, cousins, uncles, and aunts, all working together on either a full-time or part-time basis. Open every day, the Morningside Greenhouse symbolizes tried and true principles of hard work, cooperation, and a devotion to customer service.

Benjamin H. Fischer was a young man who made his dream come true. He worked at the Paterson Rose Company, which was located near the Brownstone House. As that business wound down, he started his own florist business nearby on Avenue B in Haledon. He then purchased the Morningside Greenhouse in North Haledon. Money was tight, and among the assets of the greenhouse was a supply of stationery on which the Morningside Greenhouse name was printed. Not one to waste valuable assets, Fischer adopted Morningside Greenhouse as the corporate title of his new venture.

The original greenhouse was also retained. It was erected on the firm's present location, purchased in 1945, at the intersection of West Broadway and Central Avenue in Haledon, overlooking historic Paterson.

The business flourished and grew like the wide variety of flowers and plants Morningside provides customers throughout Passaic County and beyond. Today Morningside Greenhouse is a well-rounded operation offering service for funerals, daily trade (birthdays, anniversaries, hospital patients, and spur-of-the-moment customers), parties, and banquets, as well as a brisk business in award-winning exotic plants.

Following the death of Benjamin Fischer at the age of 48, his widow, Ruth, and brother, George, persevered with the help of Benjamin and Ruth's children. Benjamin Jr. joined the business on a full-time basis after graduating from college in 1963. Brian came into the firm four years later following graduation from college.

The younger siblings also worked in the business while pursuing their separate careers. Through the years Benjamin Sr.'s sister, Pearl Soder, now 80 years of age, has been a steadfast member of the family team. In 1983 Benjamin Jr. began his own wholesale business in New York City, leaving management of Morningside Greenhouse in Brian's hands.

Looking to the future, Brian says only half of the business is oriented toward major events, such as weddings and funerals. More and more, business is directed to the walk-in "non-occassion" trade as people give flowers for many reasons.

At Morningside Greenhouse, it is always a bright spring day filled with flowers, just as Benjamin H. Fischer, Sr., wanted it.

Morningside's original greenhouse was erected on the firm's present location, purchased in 1945, at West Broadway and Central Avenue in Haledon. Photo circa 1957

MONA INDUSTRIES, INC.

Since the 1700s Paterson has beckoned to resourceful persons. Even in modern times the old Silk City still drew those willing to toil and achieve in business. Three such entrepreneurs were Dr. Karl Heyman, Walter O. Schlimbach, and Robert Sommer, who together launched Mona Industries, Inc., on August 1, 1951.

The trio worked for a company in Kearny and, as often happens in a free economy, believed they could manufacture better yarn treatment solutions than their employer. As a result, they pooled their resources and set up shop in a defunct chemical plant on East 23rd Street in Paterson. Money was tight, so the new venture took as its name part of the previous firm's name whose monogram remained on the front gate.

As often happens, what one does in the business world is different than what one had set out to do. Such was the case for Mona Industries' founders. By the mid-1950s, as Paterson's textile industry declined, Mona was forced to find new markets.

The firm's first major customer was Lever Brothers, for whom Mona produced ingredients for Lever's synthetic detergents. Thus, the thrust of the business changed to producing raw material intermediates, used by such nationally known companies as Avon, Clairol, Colgate, and others manufacturing detergents and shampoos. Specialty compounds for the personal care and household industries became the mainstay of the business, and the firm embarked on ever-expanding markets and profitability.

Ten years after the company's founding J.W. "Jack" Braitmayer, who had worked at IBM before moving into the flavor and fragrance business, joined Mona Industries, replacing Robert Sommer. Over the years he bought out the several other partners and now has controlling interest in the firm.

Looking back over the past quarter-century, Braitmayer has seen continued growth emerge as the product of his firm's commitment to people, product quality, and research and development. With Mona Industries' marketing growth came physical expansion as its facilities blossomed from East 23rd to East 24th Street, covering nearly an entire block. The company's staff now numbers more than 100 workers, many of whom live in Paterson and its surrounding communities. In addition to the work force, says Braitmayer, the area offers ready access to many of the firm's primary customers.

One of Mona's employees, Joseph Schon, a native of Czechoslovakia, came to work in the firm's Maintenance Department. Soon his ability and training came to the fore, and he became the company's chief engineer. Today he heads Mona's Schon Industries Division, providing industrial engineering expertise to other businesses.

Braitmayer credits much of the firm's recent growth to the marketing skill of its president J. Jay McAndrews, who joined Mona Industries, Inc., eight years ago from a senior marketing position at GAF Corporation. Today Mona's products are marketed worldwide.

Much of Mona's past success can be credited to its top management, which consists of (from left) J. Jay McAndrews, president of Mona Industries; J.W. Braitmayer, chairman of Mona Industries; and Joseph Schon, Mona Industries' chief engineer and head of Mona's Schon Industries Division.

When Dr. Karl Heyman, Walter O. Schlimbach, and Robert Sommer founded Mona Industries on August 1, 1951, they set up shop in this defunct chemical plant on East 23rd Street in Paterson.

CEDAR LAWN CEMETERY

Cedar Lawn Cemetery is the final resting place for thousands who built Paterson and much of Passaic County, as well as nearby Bergen County, physically, economically, socially, and spiritually. The great and the common rest together in this southwest corner of the Silk City, bounded on all sides by heavily traveled thoroughfares—Lakeview and Crooks avenues, McLean Boulevard (Route 20), and Route 46, as well as the modern Interstate Route 80.

Cedar Lawn forms an isle of tranquility in the midst of the hustle and bustle, literally mere yards from its boundaries. There is a quiet air about Cedar Lawn that is indescribably peaceful. The beautiful foliage of oak, elm, fir, and beech cast their shadows over the lush shrubbery and carpet of grass that everywhere form a beautiful and restful scene.

Prior to the nondenominational cemetery's opening in 1867—when the first interment, that of Nancy Fletcher, wife of John Fletcher, took place on September 27—burials of the dead in Paterson were made in graveyards scattered indiscriminately around the city. Many of these stood in the direct path of the city's expansion and business activity. And little or no provision had been made for their perpetual care, so many lay in great disrepair.

The Hobart family mausoleum at Cedar Lawn Cemetery, where the body of United States Vice-President Garret A. Hobart is interred.

The cylindrical Prehn family mausoleum, with its frieze depicting children, memorializes three children who died.

Cedar Lawn Cemetery was incorporated on March 28, 1865, just prior to the end of the Civil War, by a group of Paterson's leading industrial, business, and civic leaders who saw that this final resting place should be protected by proper financial arrangements and a superior topographical design.

The first concern was addressed by the incorporators who provided for a Special Fund for Perpetual Care. A portion of all fees made to the cemetery for the purchase of plots is designated to this endowment to provide ongoing care of the plots and the cemetery's grounds.

The second concern, that of the design and topographical aesthetics of the grounds, was entrusted to General Egert L. Viele, a topographical and design engineer. Cedar Lawn became one of the first in the nation to use the park concept.

By 1868 the Paterson Horse Railroad (trolley) line had been extended to the cemetery. Patersonians, in their Sunday best, would come to Cedar Lawn as a day's outing away from the busy city. The cemetery served as a park for area residents. (The

The Cedar Lawn Cemetery office building appears today very much as it did in this photograph from the 1930s.

city's first designated parks—Eastside and Westside—were not established until 1889.)

Some of the city's most prominent citizens served as the founders of Cedar Lawn, including John J. Brown, Paterson's first mayor after its incorporation as a city and the first president of First National Bank (predecessor of today's First Fidelity Bank of North Jersey, N.A.).

Indicative of the cemetery's prominence is that a good portion of those interred during its early years were the "power elite" of Paterson and its environs. They include John Ryle, "father of the silk industry" in the city; Nicholas Murray Butler, leading educator and president of Columbia University; Edward B. Haines, founder of *The Paterson News*; Rear Admiral James Entwistle of Spanish-American War fame; and the three most famous locomotive builders of their day, Thomas Rogers, Charles Danforth, and Dan Cooke.

Upon his election as Vice-President of the United States with President William McKinley, Garret A. Hobart resigned as a member of the cemetery's board of directors. His remains were returned two years later to be interred at Cedar Lawn following the Vice-President's premature death. Hobart's impressive Greek Revival-style "temple" mausoleum was designed by Henry Bacon, who also designed the Lincoln Memorial.

But Cedar Lawn then, as now, was never restricted only to the most prominent residents of the city and its surrounding communities. Indeed as many of Paterson's former cemeteries and graveyards were abandoned and reclaimed for the city's growing industries and businesses, many hundreds of these remains were reinterred at Cedar Lawn. One such graveyard at Sandy Hill, which closed around 1915, is now the site of Eastside High School, hence the school teams' nickname, "The Ghosts."

The bucolic nature of Cedar Lawn's 85 acres—nestled in the midst of the nation's largest metropolitan region—is punctuated by miniature architecture with beautifully decorated doorways and stained-glass windows. There is also an abundance of inspiring nineteenth-century monuments and sculpture, including the work of Augustus St. Gaudens and Paterson's own noted sculptor, Gaetano Federici.

As large as Cedar Lawn is in size, says superintendent William Birchenough, its available plots are decreasing. Beginning in 1968 the cemetery began offering crematoria services with its four units, and Cedar Lawn currently serves as a central crematoria for North Jersey and parts of New York. Burials average about 500 per year, while cremations number nearly 2,000 per year.

The cemetery has never employed a sales force, and today works discreetly with families, funeral directors, executors, and others in providing solace to the bereaved within Cedar Lawn's magnificent grounds. However, it is to the family and decedant's best interests to purchase plots and prepare interment instructions in advance.

"Cedar Lawn is meant as a place of rest and comfort for the survivors; We encourage those who wish to take the burden of making funeral arrangements off the shoulders of loved ones and friends during trying times. That in itself is a gift of caring."

The main gate to Cedar Lawn Cemetery opens to a park-like setting of peace and beauty today as it did more than a half-century ago, when this photograph was taken.

TREE TAVERN PRODUCTS

The Tree Tavern Restaurant's grand opening in 1934 had friend and famous heavyweight boxing champion Jack Dempsey serving the first customer as founder Louis Priore (second from right) watches.

Paterson is the birthplace of technologies and products that have become generally or popularly used in this country and around the world. Textiles, locomotives, the repeating revolver, aircraft engines, the first practical submarine, and other developments either have had their origins in Paterson or have been tied inextricably to the city.

While it is the historic cradle of American industry, Paterson is also home to a broad range of consumer products, from cosmetics to frozen foods. Tree Tavern Products, which manufactures and markets popular frozen pizza pies and other food products, was one of the pioneers of what has become an everyday convenience for millions.

The company had its origins in the 1930s, when Louis Priore, the son of immigrants, opened the Tree Tavern, named for a tree growing in the lobby. Then as now, raising capital for the business was a major undertaking—although Priore's methods were much different than those used today.

According to Louis Francia, his grandson and now head of Tree Tavern Products, Priore went to his friends and family members to collect the money he needed to set up his new business. With the country in the depths of the Great Depression, the money he raised came in the form of small amounts of cash. These he placed in brown paper bags and dutifully recorded the amounts he received right on the bags. Later, as the tavern began to make money, he paid back every dollar he borrowed and crossed off the names of those who had lent him the funds.

The tavern became a popular attraction in downtown Paterson, and Priore needed management assistance to run the business properly. As a result, he brought his son-in-law, Frank Francia, into the business.

Francia had worked his way through the evening division of Newark College of Engineering (now the New Jersey Institute of Technology). It took him seven years, but he became an engineer and worked for Wright Aeronautical during World War II. He also helped his father-in-law, and by war's end he was employed full time at the Tree Tavern, providing invaluable management and administrative support for his entrepreneurial father-in-law.

Priore and his son-in-law became an innovative team in expanding the horizons of the popular tavern and restaurant. Customers were regularly asking for take-out meals at the tavern. Priore and Francia, by the 1950s, were looking for ways of accommodating this market.

First they began supplying entrées to small bars and taverns in the area that did not have their own kitchens. Tree Tavern supplied small electric ovens to these establishments and sold them frozen entrées they could then heat and serve to their customers. So, in addition to the tavern itself, Tree Tavern had a truck route for outlying establishments.

During the 1950s the old icebox became a thing of the past, replaced by electric refrigerators in homes. These new appliances had large freezer compartments that could accommodate a broader range and bigger items. The Tree Tavern team of Priore and Francia moved into the frozen-food

Frank Francia, the founder of Tree Tavern Products.

business by supplying customers of the tavern with frozen take-home entrees. Especially popular was the tavern's pizza pies.

Toward the end of the 1950s Tree Tavern pizzas had been introduced into A&P stores in New Jersey. But the mass marketing of frozen foods was just starting, and it took time to achieve customer awareness and acceptance.

Louis Priore died in September 1960, not knowing if the frozen-food business would fulfill its promise. However, by the end of that year the company was rounding the corner to success.

Tree Tavern Products began operating in earnest by testing products and procedures—trying new equipment to expand production, which reached 12,000 frozen pies per day. Francia, joined by such stalwarts in the company as Michael DePatria, who had joined Tree Tavern as a butcher in the 1940s and is now a valued member of the firm's management team, redoubled the company's efforts.

By 1968 the frozen-food business outgrew the restaurant, which was closed to provide more production space. The following year a new plant was constructed, and Tree Tavern was on its way to filling practically the entire block between Crosby and Straight streets. Production increased to 16,000 units per day in an automated plant employing 40 people.

In 1972 Louis Francia, Frank's son and Louis Priore's grandson, joined the business after graduating from the University of Rochester. At that time frozen, convenience foods were becoming commonplace—marketed by large corporations. Tree Tavern was embroiled in a David versus Goliath competition.

With the company's introduction of a 10-ounce individual portion frozen pizza, Tree Tavern began reaching the rising "singles" market. Shortly thereafter Tree Tavern Products branched out into other specialty markets with a whole-wheat pizza sold in health food stores, as well as non-cholesterol pizzas featuring a tofu-based mozzarella cheese.

Next came stuffed potato items and the newest product, stuffed pretzels. All of these products, and those still in the planning stages, allow Tree Tavern Products to build on a foundation dating back 50 years.

Lou Francia says Paterson has a top labor supply and a central location from which the company can reach outlets throughout the Northeast. Those attributes, combined with Tree Tavern Products' commitment to service and value, add up to continued success for the firm in catering to American desires for convenient food products.

Michael DePatria, a valued member of the Tree Tavern Products management team for more than 40 years.

Former Governor Richard J. Hughes views the architect's plans for the new addition to the Tree Tavern Restaurant. The addition was made to handle the expanding frozen-food business.

PUBLIC SERVICE ELECTRIC & GAS COMPANY

In Charles A. Shriner's book, *Paterson, New Jersey*, published in 1890, he wrote that ". . . Paterson is one of the best illuminated cities in the country. . . . In many portions of the city it is as bright at midnight as it is at midday."

Today much of Paterson is brighter yet, illuminated by one of the most successful power utilities in the country, Public Service Electric & Gas Company, or PSE&G, as it is more popularly known.

Paterson's roots are in power, albeit the waterpower of the Great Falls that provided the force for late eighteenth- and early nineteenth-century manufacturing. As the city grew economically and residentially, more efficient and reliable sources were needed to power the industrial plants and light commercial and residential districts.

As early as 1825 the Paterson Gas Light Company was organized. Inexplicably it did not begin to function commercially until more than 20 years later, but Paterson Gas became the dominant power company in the city for more than 30 years.

In 1880 People's Gas Light Company began operations, but by 1882 both Paterson Gas Light and its recent competitor, People's, had been acquired by United Gas Improvement Company of Philadelphia. In 1888 two electric companies—Paterson Electric Light and Edison Electric Illuminating—began to serve the city. They also were consolidated by UGIC of Philadelphia.

With the formation of Public Service Electric & Gas Company in 1903, the Paterson gas and electric operations were folded into the new public utility. The city—and most of the county—have been served by the one utility firm ever since.

As a regulated utility providing an essential service, PSE&G is required to serve the public good. And PSE&G has served the greater Paterson area faithfully for more than 80 years. The company has led the industry in technological advances to provide the levels of service—and output of electric and gas energy—needed by the expanding New Jersey economy.

BELOW: One of PSE&G's newest facilities, the Garret Mountain District Office, is located in this West Paterson building. From this location both customer and marketing service operations for the Passaic County area are coordinated.

ABOVE: The headquarters of PSE&G's Gas Transmission and Distribution Department's Northern Division is located at 240 Kuller Road in Clifton, near the bed of the historic Morris Canal just outside Paterson.

Beyond its chartered service responsibilities, PSE&G is a dedicated corporate citizen of the state and communities it serves. The firm's community affairs programs—and economic development programs that help promote the state—broaden the beneficial effects of its presence on Paterson and New Jersey in its entirety.

The transmission and distribution of gas and electricity as the dominant forms of energy today are entrusted to the dedicated professionals of Public Service Electric & Gas Company, whose primary concerns are the people and businesses of New Jersey. Coincidentally the Paterson Falls, originally the source of the city's power, has been reharnessed to produce electricity.

ASSOCIATED FIRE PROTECTION, INC.

Associated Fire Protection, Inc., originated 40 years ago in this building, a garage at 313 Atlantic Street, as Associated Extinguisher Services. Photo circa 1947

The city of Paterson has experienced its shares of destructive fires since its founding in 1831. Structures erected in the nineteenth century were often made of wood without implementing modern building safety code requirements such as fire walls and enclosed stairwells, and were therefore highly flammable. Frequently commercial buildings were constructed in long rows, and a fire in one could mean the destruction of an entire block. Paterson's Great Fire of 1902, for example, devastated the city's downtown commercial district.

Fire protection for businesses has advanced dramatically since the days when the only available recourse was a bucket filled with water. Today sophisticated computer-based technology using advanced equipment provides life safety while preserving business assets.

For the past 40 years businesses in the greater Paterson region have turned to Associated Fire Protection, Inc., for the equipment, service, and technical means to combat fire's threats to human lives and assets.

The company, like many new ventures, originated in a garage, located at 313 Atlantic Street. John Straten, the company founder, came to the United States from Germany during the 1920s. He was employed as a sales engineer with the Walter Kidde Company.

Initially the firm was a distributor of Kidde fire protection products and devices, and its primary function was recharging and repairing portable fire extinguishers. Gradually Associated Fire Protection's responsibilities for Kidde expanded to include selling fire extinguishers, and then selling and installing automatic fire suppression systems.

Today the company provides engineering and electrical contracting in the fire protection and life-safety fields, fire suppression system service, sales of portable fire extinguishers and safety equipment, and portable fire extinguisher service. The firm sells and installs equipment and systems from such leading fire protection manufacturers as Kidde and Pyrotronics.

With John Straten's death in 1969, his son, Roland, took over management of Associated Fire Protection. Since that time the firm has experienced a tenfold increase in sales and a broadening market. Because of Paterson's strategic location in Northern New Jersey, with its major highway and transportation networks, Associated Fire Protection can quickly and effectively service the bulk of its customers within a 50-mile radius. In addition, the company has customers as far afield as Utah, Puerto Rico, and the Middle East.

Growth brought a series of relocations, culminating with the firm's settling in new headquarters at 100 Jackson Street in Paterson. Featuring ample office space as well as modern testing, servicing, and storage facilities, Associated Fire Protection's new home gives the company a strong administrative base.

With new high-cost technologies and increasingly expensive investments for businesses, the protective services and systems provided by Associated Fire Protection, Inc., are becoming more important components in the safety and risk management operations of modern businesses.

Associated Fire Protection's modern facility at 100 Jackson Street houses the firm's inventory of state-of-the-art fire protection equipment.

COLONIAL GRAPHICS, INC.

Paterson is the spawning ground of companies that provide services or manufactured products used by consumers—individuals and businesses. Their success is shown by growth and the scope of their markets, ranging from local to regional to national in character.

John V. Turi's Colonial Graphics, a color sheet, web printing, and graphics arts company, is one of Paterson's success stories. Begun as Colonial Press, a part-time letterpress shop in a house on East 29th Street, the company today, 30 years later, occupies a modern printing plant covering more than 24,000 square feet with attractive office areas for customer convenience and comfort.

Turi, a Paterson native, came into the printing trade while working part time as he attended school. Later he worked for local newspapers. From his start as a "cottage printer" in 1957, providing business forms and social and church printing and other events, Turi later broadened his commercial business with the acquisition of offset equipment. He "sold during the day and printed at night."

Despite this hectic schedule Turi devoted himself to educational and civic pursuits. He attended courses in better business techniques, while also becoming involved in such service groups as the Rotary and Jaycees, of which he became National Director and was recognized as one of the Jaycees' Outstanding Young Men.

Due to the growth of the business, Colonial relocated a total of six times to larger quarters. The company was located on East Railway Avenue and then East 18th Street, before Turi acquired his present building on Maryland Avenue in 1975. This space, a former textile printing establishment, covered 7,500 square feet, which Turi has since tripled in size.

However, physical expansion was only one facet of Colonial Graphics' growth. The firm broadened its services for marketing and sales applications by its diverse roster of clients. Four-color catalogs and brochures, direct mail, magazines and books, and point-of-purchase pieces are all produced by Colonial's computerized, high-speed, fine reproduction presses.

Colonial Graphics, with its graphics and production capability, can take virtually any printing assignment from concept to finished piece. The company is one of the few that can print, fold and trim, and carton finished material in one automated operation.

For the future, says Turi, Colonial Graphics, Inc., is being positioned for the specialized process color, high-volume printing work needed for modern sales and marketing programs.

John V. Turi, founder and president of Colonial Graphics, with his first letterpress now located in the company's modern offices and printing plant on Maryland Avenue.

John V. Turi (center) at the company's first office on East 29th Street.

The management staff of Colonial Graphics at one of the company's modern presses. In the back row (left to right) are Emily DeGise, George Conklin, and John V. Turi. In the front row (left to right) are Mike Morongell, Carl Turi, and Jay Turi.

SCHENKER, SCHENKER & RABINOWITZ

The early years of the Great Depression were not a propitious time for a young architect straight from New York University to find employment in his field. Sidney Schenker, frustrated in that quest, began his own small firm in those difficult times. Today, more than a half-century later, that architectural and planning firm thrives under the direction of his son, L. Michael, and Philip Rabinowitz, one of the many fine young architects who advanced to prominence under the elder Schenker's tutelage.

From its beginnings the firm has been a Paterson operation—first doing business on VanHouten Street, then Broadway, until finding its permanent home at 35 Church Street across from the historic Hamilton Club. Sidney Schenker, the son of Max and Rebecca Schenker, was born in the city and educated there. His roots in the Silk City ran deep.

During those Depression years the young architect struggled against the tide. He did work for Paterson's retailers, private homes, apartment buildings, offices, and any other projects he could find.

Following World War II he rode the crest of the postwar construction boom with designs for specialty retail outlets up and down the East Coast, new apartment houses, suburban shopping centers, bowling alleys and office buildings, middle-income housing for young veterans, as well as avant-garde residences in exclusive neighborhoods surrounding the New York Metro area.

Sidney Schenker

During the 1940s and 1950s his sole practice became the training ground for many young architects who now rank among the leaders in the profession. Sidney Schenker's own stature was recognized by his appointment by the governor as president of the New Jersey State Board of Architects, and his service as president of the Architects League of Northern New Jersey and as a member of the board of the New Jersey Society of Architects.

Schenker's son, L. Michael, joined the firm in 1970 following nearly 10 years of diversified architectural experience. Philip Rabinowitz also joined the firm about that time, after completing his studies at the New York Institute of Technology in Manhattan. He became a partner in 1983.

The award-winning firm has designed and supervised construction of the nationally published new School No. 9 building on Getty Avenue, conversion of the city's Rosa Parks School for the Fine and Performing Arts, alterations and a new annex for the Passaic County Jail Intake Facility, the Jewish Federation Apartments, and the Eastside High School extension. In addition, the firm lists scores of institutional, industrial, commercial, and residential projects within Paterson and along the Eastern Seaboard to its credit.

A tradition of public service, begun by Sidney Schenker, is continued by his successors, especially with work related to Paterson's historical district and the Paterson Renaissance Organization, of which Philip Rabinowitz has been a leading force.

With a background steeped in tradition, and with a knowledgeable and innovative young staff, the firm stands uniquely qualified to draw on the rich historic fabric of the city's past and to channel that knowledge toward progressive visualization of what Paterson can become in the years ahead.

Paterson was built by men and women with vision. Its future is being designed at Schenker, Schenker & Rabinowitz for beauty and usefulness.

RIGHT: The staff of Schenker, Schenker & Rabinowitz with L. Michael Schenker (left) and Philip Rabinowitz (right), in foreground.

BELOW: The new School No. 9, which was recently honored in American School & University *magazine for outstanding design.*

STORE

PATRONS

The following individuals, companies, and organizations have made a valuable commitment to the quality of this publication. Windsor Publications and the Greater Paterson Chamber of Commerce gratefully acknowledge their participation in *Paterson and Passaic County: An Illustrated History.*

AGL Welding Supply Co., Inc.
Associated Fire Protection, Inc.*
Auto Equipment, Inc.*
Barnert Memorial Hospital Center*
George Barton
Alvin G. Blau, Realtors
Bograd's*
Bragg Funeral Homes, Inc.*
Brawer Bros., Inc.*
Britt Brokerage Company, Inc.*
Broadway Bank & Trust Company*
Brogan Cadillac-Oldsmobile*
Cedar Lawn Cemetery*
Cole, Geaney, Yamner & Byrne, P.A.*
Colonial Graphics, Inc.*
De Jong Iron Works, Inc.*
Evans Hand Allabough & Amoresano
N.B. Fairclough & Son, Inc.*
First Fidelity Bank, N.A.-North Jersey*
Frech Financial Services of N.J., PA., & FL.
Peter Garafano & Son, Inc.*
Great Falls Vending Corporation*
Heterene Chemical Company, Inc.*
Horizon Bank
Hunziker, Merrey & Jones, P.A.*
Jersey Lift Truck Company*
LDL Technology, Inc.
The Malqui Agency Inc.*
Midlantic National Bank/North*
Mikola, Fierstein, Malkin, Carrabba & Testin
Mona Industries, Inc.*
Morningside Greenhouse*
New Jersey Bell*
Passaic County Historical Society
Paterson Task Force for Community Action, Inc.
Pike Construction Co.*
Power Battery Company, Inc.*
Prospect Park Savings and Loan Association*
Public Service Electric & Gas Company*
St. Joseph's Hospital and Medical Center*
Schenker, Schenker & Rabinowitz*
A.J. Siris Products Corporation*
Joseph M. Takacs
Therwell Products Co., Inc.*
Tree Tavern Products*
Twinbrook Truck Maintenance, Inc.*
Universal Manufacturing
C.J. Vanderbeck and Son, Inc.*
Westmont Home*
The Wood Press, Inc.*

*Partners in Progress of *Paterson and Passaic County: An Illustrated History.* The histories of these companies and organizations appear in Chapter 10, beginning on page 177.

SELECTED BIBLIOGRAPHY

Clayton, Woodford W. A *History of Bergen and Passaic Counties*. New Jersey, Philadelphia, 1882.

Cotz, Jo Ann. "The Catholic Church and Community Structure: Interpreting the Americanist Controversy in Paterson, New Jersey 1880-1890." 1984. Manuscript.

Cunningham, John T. A *Century of Progress*. First National Bank of Passaic County, 1965.

Harris, Howard. "The Transformation of Ideology in the Early Industrial Revolution: Paterson, New Jersey 1820-1840." City University of New York, 1985.

Heusser, Albert H. *The History of Silk Dyeing Industry in the United States*. New York: Silk Publishing Co., 1924.

Jackson-Cross Company. *Land Utilization and Marketability Study, Paterson, New Jersey*. Paterson, N.J., 1963.

Labaw, George Warne. *Preakness and the Preakness Reformed Church, Passaic Co., New Jersey*. Board of Publications of the Reformed Church in America, 1902.

Nelson, William. *Passaic County Roads and Bridges*. Paterson, ca. 1880.

Nelson, William. *Records of the Township of Paterson, New Jersey, 1831-51*. *Paterson Evening News*, Paterson, N.J., 1895.

Nelson, William, and Shriner, Charles A. *History of Paterson and Its Environs*. 3 vols. New York: Lewis Historical Publishing Co., 1902.

Price, Lynda. *Lenni Lenape: New Jersey's Native People*. Paterson Museum. Paterson, N.J., 1979.

Scott, William W. *History of Passaic and Its Environs*. 3 vols. New York: Lewis Historical Publishing Co., 1902.

Shriner, Charles A. *Paterson, New Jersey*. Paterson Board of Trade. Paterson, N.J., 1890.

Siegel, M. *The Passaic Textile Strike*. Doctoral thesis. Columbia University, 1953. (Publication #4596.)

Snyder, John P. *The Story of New Jersey's Civil Boundaries 1606-1968*. State Bureau of Geology and Topology. Trenton, N.J., 1969.

Trumbull, L.R. A *History of Industrial Paterson*. Paterson, N.J., 1882.

INDEX

Partners in Progress Index

General Index

Italicized numbers indicate illustrations.